The Me Nobody Knows

The Me Nobody Knows

A Guide for Teen Survivors

Barbara Bean
Shari Bennett

LEXINGTON BOOKS

An Imprint of Macmillan, Inc.
NEW YORK

Maxwell Macmillan Canada
TORONTO

Maxwell Macmillan International
NEW YORK • OXFORD • SINGAPORE • SYDNEY

Library of Congress Cataloging-in-Publication Data

Bean, Barbara
The me nobody knows : a guide for teen survivors / Barbara Bean.
Shari Bennett.
p. cm.
Includes bibliographical references and index.
ISBN 0–02–902015–8 (pbk.)
1. Sexually abused teenagers—Rehabilitation—Juvenile literature.
2. Sexually abused teenagers—Mental health—Juvenile literature.
I. Bennett, Shari. II. Title.
RJ507.S49B43 1993
618.92'858223—dc20
93-12624
CIP

Lexington Books
An Imprint of Macmillan, Inc.
866 Third Avenue, New York, N.Y. 10022

Maxwell Macmillan Canada, Inc.
1200 Eglinton Avenue East
Suite 200
Don Mills, Ontario M3C 3N1

Macmillan, Inc. is part of the Maxwell Communication
Group of Companies

Printed in the United States of America

printing number
3 4 5 6 7 8 9 10

In loving memory of my mother, Celia (Sadie) Bean, whose strength continues to be a constant source of inspiration to me.

To my mother, June Forrest Bennett, who died before this book was completed. Her constant, unwavering belief in me taught me to believe in myself.

To all survivors, past, present, and future for whom this book was written.

I tell the story
Somebody stole my life but I'm taking it back
I can see colors I can see colors now

Tracing the truth through the tangle of lies
Forgiving myself what I did to survive
I am living I am living

—From "Light in the Hall" by Fred
Small and Jayne Lacey

Acknowledgement for "Light in the Hall" to Fred Small and Jayne Lacey. Words by Fred Small and Jayne Lacey, music by Fred Small. Pine Barrens Music (BMI) 1989. Reprinted with permission of the authors.

A Word of Advice

Dear Reader,

This book was written as an informational resource for teenagers who have been sexually abused. The exercises and suggestions should be used under the guidance of a trained mental health professional. In no way is this book intended to replace or override face-to-face therapy. The authors and publishers will not be liable for the use, misuse, or interpretations made by those reading this book.

Sexual abuse recovery needs to be undertaken with the help of competently trained mental health professionals. For teenagers this is especially important. We strongly encourage you to get assistance in finding a well-trained and responsible therapist. We further suggest, whenever possible, that you enlist the support and aid of your parents or other concerned and safe adults to help you with your recovery.

Contents

Acknowledgments   *xi*
Introduction   *xiii*

PART I
The Beginning

1 Self, Safety, and Support   3

2 Effects of Being Sexually Abused   9

3 From Ages 12 to 21   24

4 From the Cosbys to the Bundys   30
(and Everything in Between)

5 Growing Up in a Dysfunctional Family   39

6 Sexual Abuse in the Family   45

7 Sexual Abuse by Someone Outside the Family   55

8 About Abusers   60

9 Sexuality and Sexual Abuse   68

PART II
Healing

10 From Surviving to Thriving   79

11 Remembering and Sharing the Story of Your Abuse   82

12 To Tell or Not to Tell: Breaking the Silence   *85*
about Sexual Abuse

13 Developing Self-Esteem   *92*

14 Developing Healthy Relationships   *100*

15 Confronting Your Offender   *107*

16 Should I Forgive?   *121*

17 Having Fun   *127*

18 Different Therapies   *131*

19 For Your Parents   *139*

Resources   *143*
Bibliography   *147*
Index   *149*

Acknowledgments

S hari approached Barbara with the original idea for collaborating on a book for teenage survivors in the spring of 1990. The project was undertaken out of the authors' frustration with the lack of material available for adolescents. Writing sensitively for and about survivors of sexual abuse wasn't easy. Making it relevant and interesting to teenagers was harder still.

This book could not have been completed without the help of many people. We are deeply grateful to Barbara's husband, Kenneth C. Knowlton, Ph.D., for his tireless help and patience editing and re-editing and his encouragement throughout the entire process. We thank Anne Travis Brownley, M.A.L.S. for her editing and support in the earlier phases of this project. Much appreciation goes to our colleagues, Dorothy Wheeler, Ph.D., Ginny Catalfamo, M.Ed., Andrew Young, MSW, Barbara Frame, MSW, and Darlene Corbett, MSW, for their advice, expertise, and encouragement. We are grateful for the insight and training from Daniel Brown, Ph.D., Harry Aponte, MSW, David Sacheim, Ph.D., and Elaine Loughlin, MSW, in the areas of family dynamics, childhood trauma, and hypnotherapy. Also a heartfelt thanks to Barbara's daughter, Detective Lisa Jensen of the Hunterdon County Prosecutors office, New Jersey, Sex Crimes Unit, for her helpful information. We also appreciate the many other friends and family members who gave support, encouragement and advice.

This book would not have been completed without the typing skills and patience of Roxanne Lavin. We especially thank our editor, Margaret Zuskey for her belief in the importance of this book and assistant editor Sarah Zobel for all her help. We are indebted to all the reviewers who took the time to offer their valuable input. Thanks go to the copy editor Beverly Miller and production supervisor Carol Mayhew for helping to tie up the loose ends.

Special acknowledgments go to Michael Walsh, a survivor of abuse who has become politically active in creating legislation for child victims of physical and sexual abuse; to Rebecca Nicoll for contributing her honest, straightforward teenage perspective to this book, and to Shari's teenage survivor group for letting their group sessions be published so others might benefit. We especially acknowledge all those survivors whose experiences and interviews greatly helped in the creation of this book, and from whom we have learned so much.

Introduction

At least one of four girls and one of seven boys are sexually abused before their eighteenth birthday. Being abused can make you feel different from others, make you feel unsafe and alone, cause trouble in your relationships, affect your ability to concentrate, and make you feel depressed. It creates problems that may continue for a long time. This book will help you deal with these problems.

Throughout the book we use certain words and concepts that you should understand.

Sexual abuse occurs when a person takes advantage of someone in a sexual way. If obvious, it is called *overt abuse;* if subtle, *covert abuse.*

Overt sexual abuse occurs when someone touches you or makes you touch him or her in ways that are uncomfortable to you; this can be anything from kissing to intercourse. It includes someone touching your breasts or genitals without your permission, taking nude or sexually provocative pictures of you, or making you take such pictures of them. It also includes making you participate in or watch others in sexual acts and offering or selling you for sexual purposes. Sexual abuse can include hitting, biting, and other forms of physical abuse.

Covert sexual abuse occurs when someone (usually whom you know well) is overly concerned with your sexuality and makes sexual comments, suggestions, or accusations or asks questions about your personal sexual habits. It is abuse when someone repeatedly makes comments that make you ashamed, embarrassed, or confused about yourself and your sexuality. It is abuse when someone looks at or touches you in ways that make you nervous or uncomfortable, like giving you backrubs that feel "weird." It's abuse if someone frequently walks in on you "accidentally" or without knocking while you are in the bathroom or bedroom. It can be sexual abuse even if the person never touches you. The person usually denies doing anything wrong. This type of abuse causes you to doubt your sense of reality, and you may feel guilty and crazy for thinking something is wrong.

Incest is sexual contact between family members. Different states have different laws defining it. Often stepparents and live-in lovers of a parent are considered family members.

In an act of sexual abuse there is at least one victim and one offender. A *victim* is a person who has been misled, tricked, or threatened into a sexual activity by someone more powerful. Victims can be males or females. For either, some of the ways of dealing with and healing from abuse are similar. The *offender* uses his or her position of authority or power to overcome the victim's control and take advantage of that person sexually. A victim who has lived through the abuse is a *survivor*. We think of this level as a first-stage survivor. We define people who have decided to take steps to regain control of their lives as second-stage survivors. Reading this book means you are already a second-stage survivor.

Although there are some similarities in the ways males and females deal with sexual abuse, there are some major differences as well. This is possibly in part due to society's different attitudes toward males and females: males aren't—or shouldn't be— victims; it's "unmanly" for boys to be sexually abused. There is a commonly held belief that males are "strong" and should be able to protect themselves, while females are "weak" and thus more easily victimized. If a boy is sexually abused by a woman, he is often seen as "gaining sexual experience," rather than as being victimized. If he is abused by a man he may be seen as weak or his sexuality might be questioned. Such attitudes create additional shame for boys and even more reluctance for them to acknowledge the abuse than for girls.

Cult and ritual abuse are forms of abuse that are so severe they need to be mentioned separately. Cult abuse occurs when the victim is abused sexually and physically as part of a religious ceremony. It can occur within or outside the family. Sometimes relatives are involved, and sometimes it may include more than one generation of victims and abusers. Rituals are a part of cult abuse and can include drugs, alcohol, animals, and special ceremonies. Ritual abuse can exist apart from cult abuse. It is a planned, systematic form of physical and sexual torture, involving specific activities and sometimes special tools.

Boundaries define a person's physical and emotional areas that should be entered only with his or her permission. A boundary is an imaginary line that separates your space from someone else's. You have the right to decide how near you will let others approach you physically and emotionally. You should be the one who decides when you want to be touched and when you want to talk. Boundaries change with time. For example, a parent doesn't have to ask permission to change an infant's diaper but should ask permission to enter a 10 year old's room while he or she is dressing.

The concept of boundaries includes that of *personal limits*, which means not pushing yourself further or longer than you can comfortably go. You may have gone beyond your personal limits when you find yourself frustrated, depressed, angry, or frightened. Any of these reactions could indicate that you have reached your limit for the time being and should take a break from whatever you are doing. Pay attention to your feelings; do not force yourself to continue an activity that makes you feel bad. If it's something that you do have to finish, like homework, try to find someone to help you with it.

Therapy, the process you go through with a trained counselor to help you cope with and develop a new understanding of what happened to you, can help you learn how to deal with your feelings. The goal of therapy is to help you to feel and function better. This book will work best if you are in therapy. If you are not, this book could help you to find the right therapy for you. Refer to chapter 18 for information on therapy. You can also use the book to determine whether you have been abused and to help you understand how the abuse has affected your life. You can use the book as a personal journal as well as an information source. Space is provided in most chapters to write about your thoughts, feelings, and experiences. There is also a chapter you can give to your parents explaining about abuse.

Throughout this book we include interviews, stories, and parts of group therapy sessions with teenagers who are working through their abuse. Names and all identifying information have been changed to ensure privacy and confidentiality. Due to their length, quotations have been edited, but the meaning has been left intact. Shari's adolescent survivor group, girls ages 16 and 17, agreed to share their stories and feelings in the hope of helping others.

What the Abuse Was Like

Kayla: I kept telling myself that it was all right, it was natural because he was my dad. . . .

Skylar: You want to convince yourself.

Kayla: Yeah, that this is really normal activity.

Skylar: 'Cause you didn't know how to handle it.

Kayla: 'Cause I didn't know why I was feeling so uncomfortable, so I just kept doing it!

Skylar: So you made excuses like, "Oh well, I shouldn't feel uncomfortable. . . ."

Ashley: I didn't really think about whether it was wrong or right. I just didn't want to cause problems in my family.

On Recovery and Counseling

Skylar: I'm starting to feel better now that I have people my age saying the same thing that's happened to me. . . .

Ashley: I had to talk about it so much that I couldn't deny anymore—I couldn't deny that it bothered me.

Shari: What advice would you give to other kids who were being abused?

Skylar: Don't feel so bad, it wasn't your fault, and you shouldn't be blamed. Just talk about it more, and you'll feel much better.

Ashley: I really don't view counseling as badly as I did before. You know, I even suggested my boyfriend go. I think if you get the right counselor, it's the best thing.

Skylar: Same with me. I went through so many other people and I hated them. Then finally I found Mary.

Shari: What do you think is important to look for in a counselor?

Skylar: Someone who listens to you—cares about you and gives you good advice.

Ashley: Someone who seems young enough, even if they're not young—young enough to relate to you, who understands.

Skylar: Young at heart . . . . someone who can feel the same feelings and stuff like that.

Shari: So the advice you would give to a kid would be . . .

Skylar: Talk about your feelings, your problems, your fears. Talk about what you want—what you need. Stuff like that. Make sure the therapist has good toys. It's so true; I go in there and play. It takes your mind off things. I play with her toys all the time.

For most people, adults and teenagers, talking about, thinking about, and dealing with sexual abuse brings up strong feelings. You may feel overwhelmed, scared, depressed, and angry. In case you experience any of these, it is important for you to have a *safety network* available before going further. A safety network consists of those people and things that can help you when you feel this way. The following chapter will guide you in developing a network.

PART I

The Beginning

1

Self, Safety, and Support

It's important to set up a system of safe, protective, and caring people who will give you support when you have difficulties dealing with your abuse issues. These are people who respect you physically and emotionally. They listen to you and demonstrate that they heard and understood you. They don't touch you when you don't want to be touched, and they don't force you to talk when you don't want to. They respect your boundaries.

When considering who are safe people for you, determine whether they care about you and your welfare even when you make mistakes, rather than turn away from you. Do they seem caring and supportive but encourage you to be in situations in which you feel uncomfortable or unsafe? Ask yourself if they really care what happens to you. After deciding who you want in your safety network, talk with each of them about using them for support.

We have different friends for different reasons. It's the same with safe people. You may feel comfortable talking with your best friend about your anger at your parent(s) but not about your other feelings. You might prefer telling an older cousin or a counselor about those other feelings.

Both adults and other kids can be safe people. They may be family members, friends, therapists, school personnel, or clergy. Often school counselors and clergy will make time to talk with you even if they don't already know you. They can be a good beginning in developing a safety network. You should also know about the national child abuse hot line. This is a toll-free service and won't appear on the telephone bill. It is for anyone, especially kids who are victims of sexual abuse, to call for information and help. **The number is 1(800) 422-4453.** There may also be local child abuse hot lines in your area, listed in the telephone book under such headings as "Children's Protective Services," "Child Abuse Hot Line," or "Child Sexual Abuse Hot Line." They are usually found at the front of the telephone book under the main heading "Crisis" or "Children's Services." If none of these appears in your directory, call your local child protective agency. (You can get this number from directory assistance.) You can call without giving your name. You can call for information or just to talk to someone. These numbers should be included in your file of safe people so they are available when you need them. Please refer to the "resources" list at the end of the book for other help.

Begin by making a list of people in your life whom you trust and are "safe." Next to each name, write down what makes each person safe and the kinds of things you feel comfortable sharing with them. Use more paper if you need it.

Name	Makes Me Feel Safe By:	I Can Share:	Telephone Number

Now you have a partial list of people to call on while using this book. Add to it as other people and issues come to mind.

There are other ways to be safe:

- Avoiding being alone with or having angry confrontations with the offender.
- Using relaxation exercises.
- Knowing your individual limits and respecting them.
- Creating clear boundaries for yourself.

Some of these will work better than others; use only those that work for you.

Avoid Being Alone With Your Offender

You should not have to be alone with an offender who is still offending, nor should you have to be alone with someone who makes you feel uncomfortable, although this isn't always possible. If your offender doesn't live in your home, avoid him or her as best you can. If you must see that person, try to have a trusted friend with you. If the offender does live in your home, tell your therapist, school counselor, or a nonoffending family member that you are uncomfortable being alone with that person. If you still find yourself being left alone with the offender, call the child protective services or the child sexual abuse hot line. It is important to avoid any confrontations, angry or otherwise, with your offender until you and your therapist plan it out. Chapter 15 on confrontation will discuss this in more detail.

Learn Relaxation

Knowing how to relax is important. Relaxing reduces stress and the risk of stress-related illnesses, such as heart problems and ulcers. Relaxing can help you avoid becoming overwhelmed and can give you a healthier perspective on life. The following practice will help. To do it, find a time and place when you won't be disturbed. Have a clock or watch nearby so you can keep track of the time. Plan to do this activity for up to twenty minutes.

Sit or lie down, and make yourself comfortable. Breathe in and out in a slow, even manner. Then picture a peaceful scene in your mind:

a beach, a fireplace, or clouds perhaps. Some people just see colors. Others listen to soft music. What do you prefer? _____

_____

_____

_____

_____

_____

_____

_____

_____

It may take several times before you feel comfortable doing this exercise or before you can visualize anything. Don't worry about it. Go at your own pace. Some people get help from relaxation tapes that guide them to a more relaxed place. You can find these tapes in many book and music stores. If at any time during this process you feel uncomfortable, stop. This exercise isn't for everyone.

Personal Limits

Many teenagers who have been sexually abused have learned to ignore their own internal warning signs—feelings that mean they may have reached their personal limits. Your personal limit is the line between feeling all right about something and feeling overwhelmed, angry, frustrated, or uncomfortable. Teenagers often deny their feelings or think what they are feeling is wrong. Feelings are neither right nor wrong. They exist for good reasons and often serve as warnings to help avoid harm.

Have you ever ignored your feelings and wished you hadn't? What happened? _____

_____

_____

_____

_____

_____

_____

_____

Working on the exercises in this book can cause you to remember experiences that bring back painful feelings. You need to learn how to use this book in order to be as safe and comfortable as possible. Creating boundaries for yourself is one way of developing an area of safety. How long do you think you could use this book each time before feeling overwhelmed: fifteen minutes? half an hour? an hour? Whatever you choose, stop sooner if you need to.

When will you use the book? Decide when you can be sure of having privacy for the length of time you need. You may need to try different times before you find the right one for you.

Where will you keep the book and your personal entries so that others won't be tempted to read them?

Where are you going to work with this book? For some people, home will be the right place. For others it might be during therapy or at a friend's house.

I will spend [how much time]_____

_____[when]_____[where]_____

_____ and if I need to talk to someone I will call _____

_____ or _____ or _____

Now that you've begun to understand boundaries and personal limits and have started to set up your safety net, it's time to go on. The next chapter describes how sexual abuse may have affected your life.

2

Effects of Being Sexually Abused

For some people, the effects of sexual abuse are very clear; for others, they are more subtle. Some survivors may not connect any problems affecting them with the abuse for many years. It's hard to know which problems are caused by sexual abuse and which are caused by other family dysfunctions. It isn't really important to know which problems were caused by what. Sexual abuse either causes problems or reinforces existing ones.

Sexual abuse may cause you to feel dirty and ashamed and as though you are "damaged goods." You may have been hurt physically as well. You may believe that others can see what happened to you. Having these feelings means your self-esteem was affected. If you also feel responsible or guilty for what happened, this will lower your self-esteem even more. If you have low self-esteem, it's hard to feel good about yourself and to achieve all that you are capable of:

> I'm intimidated by everything, by everyone. Certain situations I don't like I mean, I can't even go out and apply for a job. I don't feel comfortable going out. (Ashley, 17)

You may feel different from and not as good as other people. Or you may feel fake, and only pretending to be normal.

> It's like everybody thinks you're such a snob and it's the other way around. You're too shy; you feel like you don't belong. I have the biggest fears. Even with my two best friends I always feel like I'm interfering, like I don't belong there. (Skylar, 16)

Perhaps you seem to have no feelings at all. Many victims of sexual abuse, teens and adults, have told us they feel numb most of the time. Some say that life is like a movie they are watching instead of living. Others have said they feel only angry or sad, and never really happy, even when things go well. Some survivors find the only way they feel alive or good is to put themselves in risky situations: doing something dangerous, stealing, or sneaking out at night. Perhaps you find yourself taking chances that you think are reasonable but that others tell you are very dangerous.

Do you put yourself at risk? _____

What do you do? _____

_____

_____

_____

_____

Does it give you a sense of excitement? _____

Does it make you feel more alive? _____

How do you feel if you're not doing these things? _____

_____

_____

_____

Do you feel anything? _____

If you have been sexually abused, you may be reluctant to trust others or to believe that they truly care about you. Relationships, sexual and nonsexual, can be difficult. Getting close to people and sharing yourself may be frightening or confusing. You may feel lonely and isolated from others. At the same time you may be afraid to get close when you want to.

> I'm afraid to start to trust people because as soon as I give them a little tiny inch they'll destroy my trust. So I just don't trust them. (Skylar, 16)

> I think if I get too close or too dependant on a person, I know eventually I'm gonna get hurt. So I think it's really hard for me to trust anyone right now. (Jimmy, 23).

> Well, I just don't trust people that good. Like, I trust them but not 100 percent. . . . Sometimes I find it harder to trust men because of what my father did. I'm not afraid of them because I know it's not every man that does that, but I just have trouble, like, adjusting to them and getting to know people. (Michael, 13).

Sex might be an issue for you. If you are sexually active, you may have problems with sex. You may not want to be sexual—or you may have sex with almost anyone and not know why.

> Well, I have problems with my boyfriend. When I disclosed everything to him, he couldn't do anything to me. I felt gross and dirty. I felt like a whore. It's weird because I had been with him for about two years before and I was just fine. And then it became a problem. I think a lot of it was my problem. I mean, I had the problem when he touched me, I was thinking of other things. I associated everything he did with [the abuser]. I just felt dirty, so I had the problems with my boyfriend. Eventually I lost him anyway. I think it stemmed from that. (Amber, 18)

> With the other boyfriends, it was because they wanted to and I wanted to please them. I wanted to make sure they were happy with me. So that's why I did it. (Ashley, 18)

Do you have sexual concerns? _____

_____

_____

_____

_____

You may have been a victim of date rape: you were pressured or forced into having sex on a date. It's a frequent problem for many survivors, because they've believed for so long that they are responsible for everything that happens. Be aware that it is rape even if you stop protesting after saying no. It is still date rape if you agreed to have sex because you felt threatened by the person you were with.

Has date rape ever happened to you? _____

How did your date pressure you? _____

_____

_____

_____

_____

_____

_____

_____

Maybe you have problems concentrating or remembering. Some people have flashbacks or nightmares of the abuse. Some survivors have panic attacks or fears about men, crowds, or other things.

I have nightmares, a lot of nightmares. It really doesn't have anything that he did to me in the nightmares. It's just his presence. It was just terrifying. I just don't like men. I mean, I'm not a lesbian or anything! I *like* men, I'm just not comfortable around them. Like my uncles; when I was little, I would cry and cry before they could give me a hug. I mean, my parents just figured it was a phase. My neighbor's father would walk in one door and I'd run out the other and go home. I just did not like men. Even now, if I'm at a party and none of my friends are with me, I get very anxious and nervous around guys. (Amber, 18)

Do you have problems with concentration, flashbacks or night-mares? _____

_____

_____

_____

_____

Some survivors have thoughts or fears of abusing others. These common thoughts cause great distress.

> Sometimes I think about whether I could abuse a kid or not. Or I think about past things that I've done and wondered if they're okay things, like if they'd be considered by society to be okay. Even with my cousins that I babysit for, I get really conscious about how I pick them up or about how I give them a bath or if I have to change their clothes, how I do that. Because I don't want them ever to go to their parents and say I did something strange. And I don't want to do anything that anybody could perceive as strange. (Erin, 17)

Sometimes abused teenagers do molest younger children.

If you have ever done this or worried about doing it, what happened? _____

_____

_____

_____

_____

_____

If you have had thoughts of abusing and especially if you have acted on them, it's very important that you talk with your therapist about it.

Post-Traumatic Stress Disorder

The effects of abuse you have just read about are part of a group of symptoms called *post-traumatic stress disorder* (PTSD). It happens to people who have had severe emotional trauma and stress, such as sexual abuse.

Post-traumatic stress is a reaction to negative events—a car crash, fire, rape—not usually experienced in everyday life. The reaction may include the shakes, nightmares, periods of crying, or anxiety. Sometimes people don't remember the situation that led to the anxiety but experience fear, guilt, shame, or anger. When people can't remember part of the trauma, they dissociate from the experience (separate these memories and/or feelings from the rest of their lives). A person who was sexually abused will have some level of PTSD. Following is a list of symptoms used to determine if someone has PTSD.* Check the ones that you think you have.

_____ Reexperiencing the event through flashbacks, dreams, or memories.

_____ Withdrawal from other people or things or feeling detached from (not emotionally connected to) others.

_____ Feeling emotionally numb or unable to respond with feelings to other people.

_____ Intense angry outbursts.

_____ Panic attacks.

_____ Sleep problems (difficulty falling asleep, waking up a lot, nightmares).

_____ Feelings of guilt about the trauma.

_____ Trouble concentrating and/or memory problems.

_____ Remembering the trauma with no feelings attached.

Flashbacks are one of the after-effects of trauma. During a flashback, the trauma is reexperienced as though it were actually happening now. They are more intense than memories. Flashbacks occur in different ways. They may be emotional, visual, auditory, or body flashbacks. During an *emotional* flashback, you may experience in-

---

*American Psychiatric Association, *Diagnostic and Statistical Manual of Mental Disorders,* 3rd ed. rev. (Washington, D.C.: American Psychiatric Association, 1987).

tense fear, anger, or sadness, with no understanding of why. In a *visual* flashback, you may see part or all of the traumatic experience as if it were happening in front of your eyes. In *auditory* flashbacks, you reexperience the voices or sounds you heard during the trauma. Sometimes the *body* holds the memory and causes you to reexperience the pain and other physical feelings associated with the abuse. The different kinds of flashbacks can occur separately or together, and they often happen before you have any conscious memory of abuse. They may make you think you are going crazy or that you're getting physically sick.

There are two kinds of PTSD. *Acute PTSD* happens immediately after the trauma. Victims have reactions of fear, guilt, or anger. They can get the shakes or have nightmares or other problems they did not have before. With traumatic events like accidents or violent crimes, the person is able to understand that his or her reaction comes from the recent experience. Trauma such as incest may be partly or fully blocked from memory, but the reactions of disgust and self-hate still occur. The victims feel bad about themselves and don't know why.

The second type of PTSD, *Chronic delayed-onset PTSD*, happens years after the traumatic experience. The survivor experiences fears, intense mood swings, guilt, and flashbacks but may not always remember or connect these to the old experience. Chronic PTSD occurs when the person had to bury feelings about the trauma while it was going on and never had the chance to talk about it and get help. PTSD can be hidden and emerge only when therapy has begun and you have started talking about the feelings. It's common to feel as though you're getting worse at that time.

Both kinds of PTSD respond to treatment—talking about the trauma and the feelings attached to it and learning to take care of yourself both physically and emotionally. We will talk more about this in part II, Healing.

Coping Skills and Defense Mechanisms

Sexual abuse is an awful experience, made worse if you have to keep it a secret afterward and can't get help. Since kids often believe they can't tell anyone about the abuse when it's happening, they find their own ways of coping. But often these "coping skills" or "defense mechanisms" that work during the abuse become problems later.

A common way to deal with trauma is to dissociate. *Dissociating* is the process of separating your painful or unpleasant feelings from your awareness. It is separating partial or total events from consciousness. Everyone dissociates to some degree, during times of boredom or embarrassment as well as during trauma, like when you daydream in class. If you experience trauma repeatedly, you may learn to dissociate easily. This often happens during the abuse. You may remember some or all of what happened but not have feelings attached to it. You may have a lot of feelings (like self-hatred, fear, or disgust) but not remember the abuse. One teenager described dissociation in this way:

> I would look at the wall and begin crawling up inside my body, up to my brain. Then I would shoot off and leave my body behind. (Paula, 18)

Another girl said:

> I'd daydream. I'd go off into this huge fantasy daydream and when it was all over I felt so cheap and gross. I felt wicked sick. I was just disgusted. As soon as I came out of my own little world, I was real depressed and felt gross. (Skylar, 16)

Still another described going numb and not feeling anything that happened:

> I didn't have any feelings. I just block all my feelings out. It didn't matter to me. I thought, well, if this is what I have to do, this is what I have to do. Otherwise he'll [the abuser] tell Mom and Dad that I went to the mall when I wasn't supposed to or I went to Cindy's house when I was grounded. Or something stupid like that and that seemed more important to me. So I just ignored what was happening to me. (Ashley, 18)

How did you dissociate during the abuse? _____

_____

_____

_____

_____

_____

Both kids and adults dissociate to keep the memories of events and the feelings separate from each other. Trying to deal with them both at the same time can be overwhelming. During abuse, dissociation is a protective way of coping with what is happening.

> Things were just weird. I was just in this state of mind where it's like, I've gotten high before and that's what it was like. 'Cause everything just seemed like I was floating above everything, and nothing was really clear or anything. (Paula, 18)

The longer you experienced abuse, the more you probably used dissociation, and the better you got at it. You may have gotten so good at it that you now dissociate in any stressful or uncomfortable situation. Lots of abused teenagers have complained about this happening. They find themselves "spacing out" or "blanking out" and not being able to feel or remember things that are happening today, even if the abuse is long over. For some, dissociation causes learning problems in school because they can't remember and follow what is being taught.

If you dissociate, what kinds of situations cause this to happen?

_____

_____

_____

_____

_____

_____

_____

Some people find that extreme dissociation is necessary to keep the memories and feelings from becoming overwhelming. These people develop separate parts or personalities inside themselves to hold different memories and feelings. These separate parts usually develop during trauma when a child is very young, to help the child cope with and "forget" the pain. They keep the feelings and memories away, protecting the child from having to face over-whelmingly painful memories. It's similar to taking a puzzle apart and putting each piece in a separate and safe place so the whole picture is never seen. This coping skill, called *multiple personality,* is a creative way for some children to live through terrible experiences that they cannot escape, but it often becomes a problem later because it interferes with their daily lives. It is treatable with therapy, and people with multiple personality can go on to lead satisfying lives. Think of dissociation as being on a scale ranging from mild to severe. On one end is everyday dissociation, and on the other end is multiple personality:

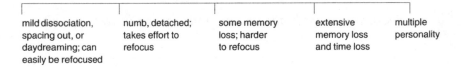

| mild dissociation, spacing out, or daydreaming; can easily be refocused | numb, detached; takes effort to refocus | some memory loss; harder to refocus | extensive memory loss and time loss | multiple personality |

Denial, telling yourself the abuse didn't happen, and *minimizing,* telling yourself that the abuse wasn't so bad or didn't mean that much to you, are common coping skills. You may have had to work hard at convincing yourself that the abuse had minimal effects, but once you did, you probably found it easier to accept what happened. Nevertheless, denial and minimizing are hurtful because they prevent you from feeling, and you need to feel in order to deal with the abuse in a healthy way.

What did you tell yourself to make the abuse more tolerable?

_____

_____

_____

_____

_____

Most kids, not only those who have been abused, find that the bad feelings they have about themselves intensify when they become teenagers. Some work hard at "proving they are good": they get good grades, have many friends, and look great on the outside. These kids are driven to be perfect, but they don't feel perfect to themselves. They use success to keep the bad feelings away. When they make mistakes, they often fall apart.

> I'm very strong, I've achieved a lot, I think. I've achieved more than most high school students have. I get straight A's, I'm athletic, I have dates, I have a boyfriend. I'm just your typical all-American kid. I've never been a black sheep or anything. I've always had plenty of friends. I've never had to worry about anything really. But I just hate failing at anything. Even getting a C. I remember freshman year was my first time getting a C, and my last time. I got a C and my parents were very pleased and they were like, "good job," you know. They never said a word about disappointment, not even one word about the C. And I was crying. I mean, it was just like I couldn't do less than perfect. I've never gotten one since because I never will go through that again. (Amber, 18)

If you are a teenager who has to be perfect, remember that you deserve everything positive you have worked for. You also deserve to have feelings—to forgive and accept yourself and to feel better.

Other teenagers hurt themselves or use drugs, alcohol, food, or sex in order to stave off the bad feelings. They may not connect feelings of depression or insecurity with the abuse. They may not even remember the abuse, but the feelings are there anyway. Some people who try to be "perfect" use compulsive/addictive behaviors—self-mutilation or eating disorders—in trying to control their lives and feelings.

> I was cutting my arms up. I still have all kinds of scars on my arms from it. I was doing a lot of crazy things. I was thinking about suicide a lot but I never really did much of anything that would make me die except for the eating disorder. I got down to eighty pounds before I went into the hospital but I had a death wish type of thing. I just was too afraid to really do it. 'Cause I thought I was going to go to hell if I did. When I was in eighth grade I was the top student in the class. I was the number one student and the teacher's pet. There was a lot of things going on at home at the time, too. So I think it was just a mix of everything that was going on and I was a straight A student, but I was having a nervous breakdown. One time there was a project due, and I freaked out. I started screaming at my mother and I was like, "God, I don't know if I can get this done." I was like a 90-year-old person, and it was only a stupid project for eighth grade. I started crying, and I couldn't stop. (Paula, 19)

If any of this sounds like you, it is important to know that you can have feelings without destroying yourself. You can get help to feel better about yourself.

We've just described ways teenagers (and adults too) control or manage their feelings. How do you control your feelings? _____

_____

_____

_____

_____

The best way to "control" feelings is to begin dealing with them rather than avoiding them through drugs, food, or work.

As you see, sexual abuse can affect almost any area of your life. Knowing which areas have been affected for you is an important step in the healing process. Dealing with your problems is the way to take back control of your life and make healthy changes.

Following is a list of symptoms, behaviors, and feelings frequently described by survivors.* We hope that going over them will show you that you are not crazy or different but suffering the effects of severe trauma. You can also use it to choose what to work on in your healing. Check the ones that apply to you and go over them with your therapist.

_____ Poor self-esteem; feelings of worthlessness or feeling unworthy

_____ Frequent or long-standing depression

_____ Suicidal thoughts or attempts, present or in the past

_____ Self-destructive behaviors, self-mutilation, often finding oneself in life-threatening situations

_____ Unexplained fears or phobias

_____ Hearing voices (this can seem like others talking, or like hearing your own thoughts)

_____ Feeling as if you are watching yourself go through the day and not really being part of the situation

_____ Unexplained discomfort or fear of certain types of touch

_____ Revulsion at the thought of certain types of foods

_____ Swallowing or gagging problems

_____ Eating disorders such as bulimia, anorexia, or binge eating

_____ Substance abuse

_____ Frequent physical problems: headaches, allergies, stomach problems, vaginal infections or pain

_____ Frequent illnesses or accidents

_____ Hating your body or feeling as though it belongs to someone else

_____ Frequent dissociation or spacing out, blanking out, or loss of time

_____ Feeling emotionally numb

*Compiled from concepts in E. Sue Blume, *Secret Survivors,* John Wiley and Sons, New York: 1989, pp. xviii–xxi, and Gerald Ellison, "Detecting a History of Incest: A Predictive Syndrome," *Social Casework* (November 1985): 525–532.

_____ Significant childhood memory gaps

_____ Feeling like a fake, as though you are playing a role

_____ Distorted reactions to situations—either too much or too little emotion for the situation

_____ Striving for perfection or control

_____ Feeling crazy

_____ Problems with anger—too much or too little

_____ Difficulties with relationships; problems with intimacy, lack of trust, fear of abandonment

_____ Continual abusive relationships

_____ Sexual issues or problems

_____ Needing to be near an escape route or sitting with your back against a wall

_____ Frequent nightmares (including dreams of monsters and threats of harm)

_____ Often feeling there is someone or something in the house when you are alone

_____ Seeing dark, shadowy figures when you are in bed at night but that usually disappear if you blink or turn on a light

_____ Hearing noises as if someone were there (footsteps, breathing, etc.)

_____ Sensation of being touched when no one is there

_____ Bed wetting

_____ Running away, fighting

_____ Frequent sexual activity with different partners

_____ Thinking about doing sexual things to younger children

_____ Touching younger children sexually or having them touch you

_____ Stealing, lying, fire setting

_____ Torturing animals

_____ Wishing you were someone else

_____ Frequently wishing you lived in a different family or had different parents

Considering all the ways that sexual abuse can affect your life may feeling overwhelming. Knowing what's normal for your age may be comforting. The next chapter deals with general teenage behaviors and feelings. You may find that in many ways you're like everyone else.

3

From Ages 12 to 21

Adolescence covers the period from about age 12 through the early 20s. At first, there are many changes in your body: breast development for girls, voice changes for boys, pubic hair, sudden growth spurts, and hormonal changes that affect your moods. Sometimes mood swings are intense: you are happy one minute and crying the next.

In early adolescence (ages 12 through 15), how peers, and especially your friends, feel about you is sometimes the most significant part of your life. This is also a time of developing relationships that may last a lifetime. Through trial and error, you're learning who to trust and how to have close friendships. You share personal information and have the other share with you. If each of you shows respect and care for what you share, trust develops, and a true friendship begins.

You might develop crushes on people of your own sex, which could be confusing or frightening. You may think about your friends and wonder what it would be like to hug, kiss, or touch them. You might talk about or act these thoughts out with your friends. This could cause mixed feelings and make you wonder about your sexuality. For many, this is just a phase of growing up. For others, these feelings continue into adulthood. (There's more about this in chapter 9.)

Depression and moodiness are common feelings. Some teenagers become so depressed that they consider killing themselves.

Have you ever felt depressed or suicidal? What was it about? _____

_____

_____

_____

_____

What did you do about these feelings? _____

_____

_____

_____

How did you keep yourself safe? _____

_____

_____

_____

In middle adolescence (ages 15 through 18) you start thinking about independence: continuing your education, making a living, having a career, getting married, and having a family. It can be a frightening as well as an exciting time. You question the authorities in your life, which can create problems, and even fights, at home. You may feel betrayed, let down, and angry. Remember that this process is normal as you move toward adulthood and independence. When you become an adult, these conflicts may be resolved.

In late adolescence (ages 18 to 21) most young adults move toward independence. Many have some idea of where they want to go and are developing plans to get there. Some go to college or to work. Some get married. This time of beginnings and endings is exciting and frightening, happy and sad. For some, struggles with parents decrease and both teens and adults begin to tolerate each other's values.

Many of your problems and concerns are common to teenagers. Most adolescents feel bad about themselves at times but find the subject too embarrassing to talk about.

Sex and sexuality are areas of concern and conflict for most teenagers (and often for adults as well). How you look and whether you're popular may be especially important to you. Making decisions about whether to have sex often comes up. If you are sexually active, you may worry about your performance.

Do you have any concerns about sex? _____ *What are they?* _____

_____

_____

_____

Have you gone out with people you didn't like because they were popular or because of peer or family pressure? Have you ever gone further sexually than you wanted because you thought you were supposed to or because your date pressured you? Have you found yourself not saying what you really feel about sex because you were afraid others will laugh at or look down on you? Have you resented others asking you personal questions that you felt pressured to answer even when you didn't want to? These are situations that teenagers often face, and confusion is common.

What situations of this sort have you been in? _____

_____

_____

_____

_____

Most teenagers go through a period when sexual matters are both exciting and frightening. Hand holding, hugging, and kissing are exciting, but going further may seem frightening or disgusting.

How do you feel about sex? _____

_____

_____

_____

Many teenagers worry about their sexual competence: how good they are at what they do, from talking to kissing and touching. Both sexes often feel they're expected to be experienced long before they are ready. They wonder whether they kiss well or are affectionate enough (or too affectionate). Either way, teenagers worry about how they come across and whether their behavior will be approved of by others.

Do you have any of these worries? _____

_____

_____

_____

If you were sexually abused and believe that no one else feels the way you do, talking to other teenage survivors is helpful because you'll see that you're not alone. There are therapy groups for teenagers who were sexually abused. Ask your therapist for information about them.

Adolescence is an unsettling time for everyone, with periods of much confusion and unhappiness. Searching for answers, developing your own values, making and changing friendships, and developing sexually all combine to create an emotional roller coaster.

Since you've begun reading this book, you've already started to find ways to help yourself.

What do you do for yourself when your feelings are overwhelming?

_____

_____

Teenagers, especially those who have been physically and/or sexually abused, may have feelings of intense anger.

If you have been sexually abused, the feelings and problems of adolescence are more serious. You have learned to push your feelings deep inside and may have no one to talk to about them. If this is the case, keep a journal or diary, and try some of the exercises in this chapter. Also, it may be a good idea for you to call the hot line and talk without having to face anyone. As we told you in chapter 1, help is available. Keep this in mind, and don't give up. You can use the next page to draw or express your feelings any way you like.

Use this space to express your anger whenever you want:

4

From the Cosbys to the Bundys (and Everything in Between)

When most people think about "a family," they think of a mother, a father, children, and perhaps grandparents. Yet many families are different from that. By "family" we mean at least one parent and one child; it may include many other relatives.

All families have problems. The number of problems is likely to increase with the numbers of people, cultures, ages, and relationships. Problems are not necessarily harmful to kids or to anyone else. What concerns us are problems that go unresolved and problems that are "resolved" in ways damaging to at least one family member. This would be considered a dysfunctional pattern; the family isn't operating well.

All families have rules and behaviors, and they can be helpful or harmful to the kids. When they're harmful, it is not always obvious to the outside world, such as the secret of sexual abuse being kept within the family.

All families share some features; all go through stages of development; all have strengths and weaknesses, just as individuals do. In some families, members care about and respect one other. They talk about their feelings and tell the truth. They don't always agree, and sometimes they argue, but each member generally feels listened to and cared about.

In other families, not everyone's rights are respected. Some members get their needs met at the expense of others. This was true in Andrea's family. Andrea lived with her mother, stepfather, and younger half-brother. When she was 11 years old, her mother was diagnosed with a brain tumor and wasn't expected to live. Shortly after her mother was hospitalized, Bob, Andrea's stepfather, began going into her bed at night and forcing her to touch him. Bob also threatened to leave Andrea and take her half-brother away after her mother died. He told her stories of terrible things that would happen to her when she was alone. As it turned out, Andrea's mother recovered, but Andrea kept the secret of the abuse for years. When she finally told, her mother attempted suicide. Andrea then had to help her mother recuperate. No one helped Andrea deal with the abuse or helped her to see that it wasn't her fault. She developed serious emotional problems and felt guilty and angry for years, until she went into therapy.

This is an extreme example of a daughter's being expected to take care of the needs of a parent while her own needs are ignored.

In all families, unexpected crises—illness, death, job loss, or moving—occur. These events create stress that upsets a family's stability. Some families appear to glide through problems, but others seem stuck. Most families fall somewhere in the middle.

Let's consider how families develop and why some do better than others. Some people marry; some choose to live together in heterosexual or gay relationships. In both cases, there is a period of adjustment when the couple get to know each other and learn to be a couple rather than simply two people sharing an apartment. They decide who is to be responsible for the day-to-day running of the household. They decide whose friends they will socialize with. Some couples talk about these issues and work them out together; others fall into patterns in which one or the other may feel resentful or dissatisfied, and issues that never seemed important may become areas of conflict.

Maybe you've already had these sorts of experiences as part of a couple. What compromises did you make? _____

_____

_____

_____

Is there anything you wish you had talked over? _____ *What?*

_____

Some couples look at and deal with problems that arise. They talk to each other about things that bother them, and their mutual respect and trust make it possible for them to reevaluate their opinions and compromise. Couples who don't talk about problems or trust each other enough find resentments building and problems going unresolved.

When a couple has children, they enter another stage when new and different decisions are required, and their expectations of each other change. Are both parents going to work? How will they split child care? How will they handle household chores? How will they deal with grandparents? The new parents now have to consider not only each other but also the wider group of relatives.

At first, parenting is usually pretty straightforward. Babies need to be kept clean, fed, healthy, happy, safe, and loved. But as they grow, they make more demands. They want to explore; they develop their own likes and dislikes and express them. As children grow, they develop their own ideas that may not agree with those of the parents. Parenting thus becomes more difficult, and the parents need to develop new ways of dealing with the changing child.

In most families, the kids are allowed to be kids and to focus on the process of growing up. They are not pushed into taking on parental roles and are not expected to take care of their parents' emotional or physical needs. When they are older, however, parents can count on them to assume appropriate responsibilities in unusual situations such as illness or an emergency at work. In these households, family rules are clear and consistent but flexible. (In single-parent families, the children may have more responsibility, but there are still clear limits to what those are.)

Typically all siblings fight, but generally they protect and genuinely care about each other. If one child knows about a situation that could be dangerous to a sibling, he or she might decide to tell their parents. Because the information was told out of caring, any resulting anger usually can be worked out, and the siblings can remain friends. In other families, conflict between brothers and sisters is strong, and the siblings are in competition for their parents' approval. They often try to get the others in trouble.

Are there are any situations in your family when you or one of your siblings told your parents about something, either because of concern for a sister or brother's safety or out of anger? _____

What happened? _____

_____

_____

_____

_____

How do you feel about it now? _____

_____

_____

_____

_____

Most parents occasionally complain about each other but don't allow the children to take sides in their marital problems. When such parents have disagreements, they are still able to continue effective parenting. The boundaries in these families, even if the parents are divorced, are clear and appropriate. The family rules are understood, everyone's role in the family is clear, the parents are in charge, and all know what is expected.

Sometimes children play one parent against the other, and a parent who has issues with a spouse or an ex-spouse may use the children against the other parent. These patterns need to be recognized, talked about, and changed. In healthy families, issues are dealt with, even if it takes a while for the situation to change. When parents have the ability to separate their marital issues from their parenting issues, they have a much better chance of resolving problems.

Other families are inconsistent and unpredictable. Behavior can change without warning. For example, you might come home to find your mother in a good mood, but when you attempt to talk with her later, she yells at you. Still later, she might complain that you never talk to her. This inconsistency would be confusing. Some families are consistent but rigid and violent:

> My father was very, very rough. He was very strict. He had this major thing against my sister because she was starting to get older and she could never go out. My father would make her stay home and iron. He would do it just to piss her off. And he would yell at her and scream at Tony, my brother. Often times, he would hit Tony just a little too hard. I remember one time, Tony was somewhere, and he was supposed to be home. He picked up my brother by his chest, by his shirt, you know, and pushed him right against the wall. He just nailed him right against the wall and started screaming at him. That was really awful. I don't remember too many happy times with my father. I used to sit at the kitchen table and we couldn't laugh and we'd try real hard because we were all giggling all the time, you know. And he would get so mad. He would just be like, "No laughing at this table!" He would scream at us. He always sent us to our rooms. He was very, very strict. (Tina, 16)

Some families are so inconsistent that kids never know what to expect from one day to another or even from moment to moment. One minute everyone could be having a good laugh, and the next dad might become angry and throw things or hit someone. Living in an unpredictable situation is so common in some families that teen-agers in them learn to expect the unexpected and become overly alert and watchful, always waiting for something to happen. They can't trust that nice people won't become mean, and they constantly hope that mean people will become nice. They don't usually talk to each other about their feelings, and feelings are not expressed openly. Some may show their feelings without concern for the others. Others may be punished for expressing feelings. If you get upset in such a family, you don't often get listened to. In fact, the others may ignore, make fun of, or get angry with you rather than talk about the situation. If this happens repeatedly, you may hide your feelings and eventually "numb out." Feelings, however, don't stop; you learn to repress them, and later you can't retrieve them easily.

Describe the ways your family behaves. _____

_____

_____

_____

Some families have rigid unspoken rules restricting members' behaviors, typically to protect one or two people in the family. In Peter's family, his mother's drinking was out of control. She would disappear, sometimes for days at a time. Peter's father and the kids would go out looking for her. They often found her passed out in the street and carried her home. Their father never discussed the drinking with them. Peter and his sister learned not to talk about it, but everyone in the neighborhood knew. Having to hide how they felt and to keep this secret made them feel guilty and confused. In their family the unspoken rules were:

1. Don't let Mom know you know she was drinking.
2. Don't let Mom know her drinking bothers you.
3. Don't tell anyone about Mom's drinking.
4. Don't let anyone see you upset.

By following these rules, the mother's secret was protected at the expense of the children's feelings and well-being.

Drinking is only one example. Anything that has unspoken rules attached to it—drugs, sexual or physical abuse, or chronic illness—can have similar effects.

In some families there may be no hitting or sexual abuse and no alcoholism or chronic illness but problems nevertheless. They can cause some of the members to feel guilty, bad, or insignificant. In these families there may be lack of respect and devaluation of one another. Sometimes feelings come out as insults: "You're so stupid," "Don't be such an idiot," "You'll never amount to anything." Sometimes feelings are expressed by giving one person too much responsibility but little credit for the work he or she does. Kim had to come home from school every day, watch her younger brother, make dinner, and clean the house, and she still got yelled at and called lazy when she wanted to go out with her friends.

How are feelings expressed and how is responsibility handled in your family? _____

_____

_____

_____

_____

_____

_____

_____

Dysfunctional families may give some members a lot of support and others very little or none. Often the one who gives the support doesn't get any in return. There is a lack of protection in these families. Kids can't count on their parents to protect them from harm. Kids don't often feel they truly belong. People in these families don't like themselves very much. They don't feel good about their relationships and are often angry or depressed. They may blame outside causes for problems or even deny that problems exist.

Following is a list of problems that can occur in families. Check those that pertain to your family, and count them. Then look at the scale after the list to see where your family falls. Most families tend to fall around the middle. (It might be helpful to do this exercise with your therapist.)

_____ Do family members stop talking to one another for long periods of time?

_____ Do family members often fight with one another?

_____ Do the kids in your family take care of the adults much of the time?

_____ Are your family's rules rigid (unable to be changed as circumstances change)?

_____ Are there unclear rules in your family?

_____ Are there unspoken rules in your family?

_____ Do the kids in your family have frequent, serious fights?

_____ Do the kids in your family often try to harm one another or get one another in trouble?

_____ When your parents fight, do they attempt to have you choose sides?

_____ Do you find it hard to predict how your parent(s) will behave from day to day?

_____ Does anyone in your family frequently abuse alcohol or drugs?

_____ Does your family deny obvious problems?

_____ Do family members, including parents, regularly insult one another?

_____ Does your family have secrets about addictions, illnesses, or previous relationships?

_____ Do family members frequently lie to one another?

_____ Does your family tend to stick to itself, avoiding outside socializing?

_____ Is there threatened or actual violence?

_____ Is it against unspoken family rules to disagree or show anger?

_____ Is there very little praise but a great deal of criticism?

_____ Has any family member made a suicide attempt?

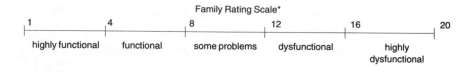

Family Rating Scale*

1		4		8		12		16		20
highly functional		functional		some problems		dysfunctional		highly dysfunctional		

If your family has many unresolved problems, you may use denial to relieve the pain you live with. You may have become upset or angry while reading this chapter. If so, call someone from your safety page, or do some relaxation or write about your feelings. _____

Growing up can be a painful and sad process. You won't be able to change or fix your family, but you can begin to heal yourself by becoming aware of the problems, setting goals and limits, and getting in touch with your feelings, and learning to take care of yourself. Your family may not accept the changes you make. They might even see you as the problem for trying to change. But you have the right to change and to choose to be a different kind of person from your parents. And you can choose to create a healthier new family when you grow older.

*The numbers on the scale refer to the number of items checked on the list.

5

Growing Up in a Dysfunctional Family

Many of your needs may not get met if you are growing up in a dysfunctional family. Your privacy could be invaded; your feelings may be ignored. There might be consequences if you express your needs. If you learn to distrust people and do not feel comfortable in social situations, your entire life will be affected. Maybe you have built a wall around yourself and never let anyone inside. You could be extremely lonely. Or you may look for affection from people who might take advantage of you or involve you in dangerous situations. You may have intense feelings that you need help with. If your parents can't control their own feelings, it will be hard for them to help you with yours. If you live in an unpredictable family where anger can explode suddenly, you learn to be alert and watchful. You anticipate blow-ups, drinking bouts, violent behavior. You learn to distrust the behavior of others, to be suspicious of what they say, and to keep secrets.

You can feel better about yourself, but you have to learn how. Therapy can help. So can social groups at school or church. Self-help books like this one can be useful. In an extreme situation, you may leave your home and live with another family. Sarah was sent to a foster home when her mother threw her out and her father was unable to provide a structured and safe home for her.

I started learning very slowly. My father was very understanding. My foster mother worked and worked with me. She would basically never let me fall down; she always held me up. I started learning how to care about people. I finally learned that secrets weren't okay. It was like I had to learn all the values again because I had no idea about anything. I had no idea what it was to take care of myself. Basic needs like eating, even though I knew how to do it, it was like I had to be told. I was sixteen years old. My foster parents put no responsibilities whatsoever on me except school. My only responsibility was cleaning my room. They started me out with basics. They started me out like a little child again—saying it was okay to do things; let me go out for pizza, let me have friends. I was only supposed to be at my foster home for two weeks. I ended up there for two and a half years. They decided they loved me after all! Slowly, very slowly, I started realizing what it was to have somebody care about me. (Sara, 19)

If you're living in a dysfunctional family, you probably experience guilt and shame. If you don't feel valued and are criticized or ridiculed by those you depend on, you're likely to think any problem is your fault. This can make you feel guilty and worthless. If you do, you probably also think you deserve the treatment you're getting. It's easier to feel guilt and shame than to feel helpless and out of control. Unfortunately, if you feel worthless, you tend to attract people who treat you as though you were worthless.

What kind of people do you attract and how do they treat you?

_____

_____

_____

_____

_____

_____

When mistakes are defined as bad, you become afraid to take risks. In a dysfunctional family when you make a mistake, anything can happen. In this situation, you may either become an overachiever or find it difficult to try anything new. Some kids think if they can't guarantee success, their only choice is not to try, but this path can keep them from becoming successful at anything, and they may end up feeling even worse about themselves. Other kids try to do everything perfectly to avoid criticism. Their choices are also limited. They do only what they know they can do well, by practicing or studying extremely long hours. If they don't do as well as they want to, they can fall apart. In dysfunctional families children aren't encouraged to learn from their mistakes; in more functional families, mistakes are seen as part of growing and learning.

Happy, confident adults know that making mistakes is part of learning. They accept their own mistakes without hating themselves for making them.

What are the beliefs about mistakes in your family? _____

_____

_____

_____

_____

When I make a mistake I feel _____

_____

_____

_____

_____

Have you ever made a mistake that you learned from? _____

_____

_____

_____

_____

In dysfunctional families, there are unspoken but clear and rigid rules that shape the way family members behave around others: Claudia Black, a therapist, developed the following concept of rules common to alcoholic families:

1. *"You must never tell anyone our business; what goes on in our family stays here."* This means you aren't allowed to tell anyone about the problems you have at home. You can't explain that your homework was torn up by an angry or drunk parent. You can't let anyone know that you didn't ignore your schoolwork but were up all night coping with a family crisis. You can't tell anyone the reason you're so tired all the time is that your father wakes you up every night and sexually abuses you.

2. *"Don't tell anyone how you really feel, because your feelings don't count."* If you grow up with the message that your feelings aren't important, you're going to believe that *you* aren't important. This makes it hard to have honest relationships since you can't share what you think or feel. You might feel different from others and like a fake. You could have trouble making true friends. If your family didn't help you develop positive feelings about yourself, it's still possible to develop them through a supportive relationship with another person—a teacher, a therapist, a friend, or a friend's parent.

3. *"People can't be trusted, so always have your guard up."* If your parents have a hard time trusting others, you will learn that outside people can't be trusted. If your parents are violent, sexually abusive, or inconsistent, you'll learn not to trust them. If you were sexually abused outside the family, you may not be able to trust your family enough to go to them for help. As a result, you may feel angry, abandoned, and isolated. If you can't trust anyone, you're likely to feel lonely and scared, but you're not allowed to let anyone know. Eventually you may be depressed and feel disconnected from the world in general.

If you haven't learned through your family how to trust, there are other avenues for learning. Getting into therapy and building a positive relationship with your therapist, developing a relationship with clergy from a local church or synagogue, starting a friendship with a teacher or adviser, or joining a local youth group can be a step toward developing helpful relationships.

If you were abused by a family member, you certainly need help, yet the unspoken rules—you can't tell anyone, you can't trust anyone, and your feelings don't count anyway—make it very hard to reach out for help.

Does your family have unspoken rules? _____What are they?

_____

_____

_____

_____

_____

_____

_____

_____

_____

_____

If you grow up feeling unsafe, so much of your energy is used being watchful that you don't have any left over for learning and growing. If you grow up feeling worthless, you don't develop the confidence needed to become a happy, self-assured adult. You are afraid to try new things for fear of making mistakes.

You can't change your family and you can't change the past, *but you can take charge of changing yourself now.* Deciding to change and to help yourself may be a frightening idea for you. You may be afraid to change if you don't know what to expect. Familiarity with what you know, even if it's painful, may seem preferable. You may be fearful of setting yourself up for disappointment.

We'll end this chapter with an "if" exercise.

If you were to change some things about yourself or for yourself, what would they be? _____

_____

_____

_____

_____

_____

_____

_____

_____

_____

_____

_____

_____

_____

_____

_____

_____

_____

6

Sexual Abuse in the Family

Perhaps you have been, or are now being, sexually abused by someone in your family. You may even think that you caused this treatment. Kids often feel responsible for the things done by the important people in their lives. If you take this responsibility, you're likely to feel ashamed and guilty.

Sometimes the sexual experience feels good or loving, or both, and that pleasure could later make you feel even worse. You may interpret your sexual arousal as proof of your guilt. *Although it's natural for your body to become aroused, the abuse is not your fault.* It can feel good to get a demonstration of affection from someone you care about. Maybe this is the only way you're shown such attention. Maybe you feel sorry for the offender and want to show him or her affection. *You still aren't at fault.*

The offender may say you caused the abuse, and maybe you believed him or her. But offenders often say that. As the child, you are put in the position of taking care of the offender's needs. This reverses your roles, since you, in effect, become the adult—a common pattern in dysfunctional families.

Sexual abuse within a family is called *incest,* and it frequently occurs in families that exhibit certain characteristics. (It continues as a pattern in some families from generation to generation.) The following questions can help you to see if your family has features commonly found in incest families. (Some of the questions are repeated from those in chapter 4, since these matters relate to many kinds of family dysfunction.)

1. Does your family have secrets about addictions, illnesses, or previous relationships? _____What are they? _____

_____

_____

_____

_____

_____

_____

2. Is there lying and dishonesty between family members? _____

About what? _____

_____

_____

_____

_____

3. Does your family tend to stick to itself, avoiding outside socializing? _____ How do they avoid outside contacts? _____

_____

_____

_____

_____

_____

_____

4. *Do they deny obvious problems such as alcohol or drug abuse?*

_____ *What are the problems, and how are they denied?* _____

_____

_____

_____

_____

_____

5. *Is there actual or threatened violence?* _____ *What kind of violence or threats?* _____

_____

_____

_____

_____

_____

6. *Does a parent or guardian tell you sex is wrong and yet behave sexually with you?* _____ *What happens?* _____

_____

_____

_____

_____

_____

7. Does any other family member behave sexually with you? _____

Who? _____

How? _____

_____

_____

_____

_____

8. Does anyone in your family behave rigidly moralistic and religious with others yet act seductively with you? _____

How? _____

_____

_____

_____

_____

_____

9. Do you feel responsible for the physical or emotional well-being of the adults in your family? _____ How? _____

_____

_____

_____

_____

_____

_____

10. *Could the same behavior be rewarded one day and punished the next?* _____ *Write down an example* _____

_____

_____

_____

_____

_____

11. *Are there other ways in which your family is unpredictable?* _____ *How?* _____

_____

_____

_____

_____

_____

12. *Do you and your siblings get pulled into your parents' arguments?* _____ *What happens?* _____

_____

_____

_____

_____

13. *Do the unspoken family rules say you must not disagree or show anger?* _____ *What happens if you do?* _____

_____

_____

_____

_____

_____

*14. Are one or both parents unavailable to you because of alcohol,
work, or illness?* _____ *Give an example.* _____

_____

_____

_____

_____

15. Is there little praise but much criticism? _____ *How does it
make you feel?* _____

_____

_____

_____

_____

The more questions you answered "yes," the more characteristics
your family shares with incest families.

Some families belong to religious or satanic cults that use sexual
abuse as part of the rituals. These cults may include extended family
members and people from the community. They also have a genera-
tion-to-generation pattern of sexual abuse. Their activities are secret

from the general population. The sexual and physical abuse they practice can be very severe. There are also families that practice ritual abuse, which is not religiously oriented, as in Michael's story:

> It was my father. Well, my ex-father. All I remember is he hooked stuff up to an electrical socket and plugged handcuffs up to it then he put them on me. He did that two times. He used to punch and kick me around and stuff. And he used to chase after us in clown costumes with knives and stuff saying these weird things. He threatened that if I told anybody, my whole entire family would end up in a graveyard that he dug out back of his house. My grandfather's house, I think it was. (Michael, 13)

Some of the effects of the abuse depend on the relationship between you and your abuser. Let's discuss various relationships.

Offenders from the Extended Family

Your extended family includes aunts, uncles, cousins, and grandparents.

You may not want to say anything because of the relationship between your family and the offender. You may think that no one will believe you. You could be worrying about hurting your parents' feelings. You might think that everyone knows and accepts it. Often these fears are groundless. Sometimes, unfortunately, they're not. Paula's family illustrates perpetrators from this group.

Paula always remembered her older cousin's grabbing her breasts and pubic area. She didn't tell her parents because the families were so close, and she thought she might get in trouble. It wasn't until she was 17 and began having memories of her uncle's raping her at age 6 that she told her parents about the abuse. They believed and supported her. She no longer goes to family functions if her cousin or uncle is there.

Grandparents as Offenders

If a grandparent sexually abuses you, this situation is likely to cause you a great deal of conflict and confusion. You may be extremely reluctant to tell anyone. Maybe you are afraid your parents won't believe you. They may not. But it's in your best interest to tell them anyway, even if you have a strong family loyalty, as in the following example.

Samantha's grandfather began having sex with her when she was 6 years old; it continued until she was 12. Samantha often looked for companionship and attention from her grandparents, but she hated the abuse. She didn't tell her parents until her grandfather died; she was afraid of breaking up the family and hurting her grandmother and also afraid of being called a liar or blamed for causing the abuse. When Samantha finally told her parents, they believed her.

Abuse by Older Siblings

You can have the same feelings and fears if the abuser is an older sibling. In addition, you may look upon him or her as your protector, especially if your family is seriously dysfunctional. You could confuse the abuse with love and care, as John and Norma did.

John felt very close to his older brother. One night when John was 12, his brother went into John's room and forced him to have sex. They never talked about it with anyone, including each other, yet they continued to have sex together, with John sometimes initiating it. This pattern continued for some time. Not until John went into therapy for other reasons did he realize this activity was sexual abuse, and it had caused many of his problems.

Norma always considered her older brother, Jim, her protector. When he began touching her sexually, she was confused and hurt. But she loved him very much and went along with the abuse, although she didn't like it. Jim first begged her not to tell their parents, and later he threatened her. When Norma was older, she finally did tell, but her mother's reaction was a concern that no one else find out. Norma's parents continued to invite both her and her brother for family dinners. Norma felt unsupported and unsafe at her mother's house.

Parents or Stepparents as Offenders

Abuse by a parent or stepparent is often the most difficult situation to cope with. The very person who is expected to care for you is instead using you for his or her own needs. As we said earlier, children need nurturing in order to develop and grow properly. A parent who sexually abuses you is not nurturing you. Instead, that parent is demanding that you take care of him or her. You are forced into an adult role.

If the abuse is by a parent, you probably blame yourself even more than if it were by some other family member. Everyone wants to love his or her parents. But instead of being able to go to your parents for help and support during confusing times, you are expected to help and take care of them. Maybe you're told you are being ungrateful or disloyal if you complain. This can distort your sense of reality or make you feel "crazy." Your reality can also be warped if the abuse is covert, as in Joan's case.

Joan was the oldest of four children. Her father always paid special attention to and confided in her. He told Joan about his marital and sexual difficulties and often complained about her mother's "frigidity." He described to Joan how she should act sexually to be a "proper" wife when she grew up. These intimate conversations made Joan, only 11 at the time, feel special. She felt she had to take care of both her parents. When she was older, she had problems with sexual relationships and with intimacy. Her father's behavior is considered very seductive, even though no touching was involved. It can lead to many of the same effects as overt sexual abuse.

The most commonly documented form of parental abuse is abuse of stepdaughters and stepsons by stepfathers. The next most common is abuse of daughters and sons by fathers. Also known, but least reported, is incest between mothers and sons or daughters. Abuse by mothers is often masked as caretaking. These mothers may give daily enemas and internal examinations. Nancy's story is an example of this kind of abuse.

Nancy's abuse started when she began dating at 12 years old. Every time she came home from a date, her mother examined her body for any marks and gave her an internal examination to see if she was still a virgin. This continued until Nancy got married at 17.

Who was your abuser and what was your experience? _____

_____

_____

_____

_____

_____

_____

_____

_____

If you are being sexually abused, you might think that everyone knows and accepts what is happening to you. Sometimes they do, but often your parents (or the nonoffending parent) don't. Try to tell your parent(s) about the abuse. They may believe and support you. This is what one survivor said:

> I think I might have been in sixth or seventh grade, and I said, "I hate my father! I just hate him." And the teacher told me to stay after school. He said, "Tina, why do you hate your father so much?" I remember being very uncomfortable, and then I just spilled my guts. He asked if there was abuse, and I said yes. He said, "Sexual?" and I was just like, "Yea," and I put my head down. He advised me to tell my mother. I told my mom, and she kicked him out. I think I sort of had a lot of guilt since I told my mom. She wasn't mad at me. She believed me and she was totally on my side. (Tina, 16)

What if your parent(s) don't believe and protect you? Tell a friend, a friend's parents, your therapist, a teacher, or some other adult who can help. Keep telling until you get some help. Call the children's sexual abuse hot line or child-at-risk hot line and speak to a counselor. You can speak to them anonymously if you want. If you aren't sure whether you are being or have been abused, the hot line counselors will provide more information and help in understanding your experience.

7

Sexual Abuse by Someone Outside the Family

Sexual abuse by someone outside the family can be as harmful as abuse by a relative. Abusers can be neighbors, friends, or authority figures. They can be of either sex or any religion or profession. Almost anyone could be an abuser.

Abuse happens because the abuser has access to kids. It happens because no one suspected this person would ever hurt a kid. It happens because the offender is considered trustworthy. It happens because abusers are good at picking out kids who are lonely or need affection. Sometimes it continues because people who know of the abuse keep it a secret. They do this for different reasons—to avoid scandal, perhaps, or to protect the offender or the offender's family. And it occurs in different ways. Perhaps the babysitter gives you kissing lessons, your neighbor fondles your buttocks, or a friend's older brother offers to drive you somewhere if you let him touch you. *This is all sexual abuse.*

Sexual abuse by strangers also occurs. The person who finds and molests you while you are alone and the man who tries to get you into his car are in many cases *pedophiles*—adults who are sexually attracted to children. They hang around playgrounds, schools, and other places children frequent.

But most sexual abuse that continues over time is from people you know. Parents and schools teach you to be wary of strangers, but they often don't teach you to be careful about people you know. More likely, you were taught to respect your elders and to obey authority. But were you also taught to listen to your own internal warning system?

If an authority figure or a family friend abused you, you may not have told. The abuser may have convinced you that *you* caused it to happen. No matter what the circumstances of the abuse, it cannot be overstressed that *you were not to blame. The adult is always responsible.* Perhaps you thought you wouldn't be believed; possibly you were afraid of being blamed; maybe you didn't want to cause trouble or hurt anyone's feelings.

> He would tell me that if I told my parents, everyone would be mad and that my mom would be upset. Everybody would just be upset, so it would be my fault for telling. I felt really gross saying it. You know I didn't want my mother to blame me because I was such a good little girl. I really was good, and I didn't want her to blame me, because he said she would. You know he was 17, and I was 8 years old. Who is she going to believe? I couldn't say he "abused" me because I didn't know what that was. I mean, I was just very embarrassed to say where he touched me and how he did it. So that's why I didn't tell. (Amber, 17)

There are many reasons for not telling about sexual abuse. What were yours? _____

_____

_____

_____

_____

_____

_____

Sometimes abuse can begin so subtly that at first you don't realize it's happening; the next thing you know, it has gone too far. By this time, you may be convinced that you led the abuser on and that you are responsible. The next story shows how this can happen.

Jeff was a 14-year-old honor student when his widower father remarried. Jeff was afraid that his relationship with his father would change. A teacher from his school, a woman in her forties, would talk to him about his feelings. Jeff willingly met with her outside school and on several occasions went home with her to talk. The teacher was concerned, she said, that the situation would affect his grades, so she offered to tutor him. She did more than that. The sexual abuse began slowly. At first the teacher would touch him subtly. Then her touches became increasingly sexual. She would sit very close, rubbing his back and neck and showing him more affection than a teacher should. Eventually they had intercourse. Jeff was positive that he had caused the "affair." The guilt he felt over it, along with his original problems, caused Jeff to fail most of his subjects. His father didn't understand what was happening, and their relationship deteriorated. Jeff became suicidal because he felt he had let everyone down. He hadn't told his story because he had believed that he caused the abuse. He also felt responsible for the teacher's feelings. It took a long time and a lot of therapy before Jeff stopped feeling responsible.

Another example of how abuse can start subtly is found in this story.

Beth liked the school bus driver who always had a smile for the kids and sometimes took them out for pizza. He was fun to be with and very affectionate—not always serious like some adults. But one day his "friendly" hugs began to feel too hard and lasted too long. She didn't say anything at first because she couldn't believe that he would do something bad. She didn't believe it until his touches began to include her buttocks and breasts.

If the offender is a neighbor or close family friend, it may be hard to believe the abuse is occurring. Sometimes the relationship between the abuser and the family makes telling hard.

It started with a friend of the family. I was also abused by a neighbor. I thought it was normal. I didn't really find out it was wrong until I was 18 and a junior in high school, and I didn't get help until I was a senior. Right now the offender and I are just not bringing it up. There's times that I could confront him with it, but I don't want to hurt my parents. I think that's what's really holding me back. (Jimmy, 23)

The offender may have a good reputation and be trusted in the community. Because of that, you may convince yourself that you caused the abuse.

> I just remember trying, like, so hard to make myself look bad. I thought it was my physical appearance, you know. I remember getting a haircut when I was about 8 or 9 and I looked like I was about 15. The way [the stylist] did my hair, I really looked like it, and I remember that day he [the abuser] was feeling me, and I thought, "Amber, you idiot! You shouldn't have come over here after getting that haircut. You're so stupid. You just set yourself up." So, I remember just trying to make myself look really bad. So, I blame myself for a lot of it, I think. I still do. (Amber, 17)

Mr. Jones is another example. He was considered the neighborhood grandfather. All the kids loved him. He would invite them to come to his house for milk and cookies in the afternoons. He picked certain "special" kids to come over by themselves. Then he would show pornographic movies and act out the movies with them. The kids later reported they didn't like the movies or the touching, but they continued to go to his house because they liked Mr. Jones.

When the abuser is a close and trusted family friend, the abuse can feel much the same as being abused by a family member. Meredith used to enjoy sleeping over at her parents' friends' house until one night when the husband came into her room and fondled her. She convinced herself that nothing had really happened. But he continued to do this when she slept over. He told her that she didn't tell because she liked it. And he also said that if she told, everyone would know how much she liked it. They would all blame her. Meredith went through a lot of confusion before she finally did tell.

When the facts finally come to light and the secrecy is broken, it is common to discover that an offender has a long history of abusing children. The person may have been considered trustworthy but nevertheless have abused many children before.

Entire families, not just kids, sometimes feel shamed and choose to keep quiet about abuse. We know of cases in which schools, churches, and hospitals have allowed a known offender to resign quietly rather than expose the institution to scandal. Such a conspiracy of silence, however, actually allows many abusers to continue abusing.

What can you do to keep yourself safe from sexual abuse in the future? Listen to your internal warning system. Get help and advice from a trained counselor. Tell what was done to you. Name names, and, if you can, have that person stopped. Refuse to belong to the conspiracy of silence.

I coauthored legislation to protect children in court because the court's trying to decide whether I should visit my father, and I know whether I should or not, not the court. (Michael, 13)

Perhaps you have other ideas. _____

8

About Abusers

Survivors of sexual abuse commonly want to make sense out of the trauma. Why were they abused? Why do some people abuse? While we don't know why your offender abused you, we can give you general descriptions of different types of perpetrators. We will use the words *abuser, offender,* and *perpetrator* interchangeably to refer to a person who sexually abuses.

Common Myths About Adult Offenders

- Child molesters come from poor or minority families.
  False. It was once thought that abusers were poor and not well educated. We now know that they come from all populations and all walks of life. They can be teachers, doctors, clergy, or janitors.

- All sexual abusers are men.
  False. Approximately 24 percent of male victims and 13 percent of female victims are abused by females acting alone or with a male partner.* Offenders may be babysitters, teachers, even mothers. Abuse by a mother is often disguised as caretaking.

*David Finklehor, *Child Sexual Abuse: New Theory and Research* (New York, Free Press, 1984), p. 173.

- Sexual abusers don't have sexual relationships with adult partners.
  False. Many perpetrators are in adult relationships and may even be in long-term marriages.
- All abusers are pedophiles (adults who desire sex with children).
  False. Pedophiles account for a small percentage of all reported cases of sexual child abuse.
- Child molesters are sexually frustrated people.
  False. Sexual abuse is not only about sex. It is also about power. Abusers exercise power over their victims and play out power sexually. Often abusers have been physically, sexually, and/or emotionally abused as children or adolescents and feel powerless. Abusing someone younger or weaker gives a sense of power, but only temporarily; offenders tend to abuse again and again.
- All sexual abuse involves alcoholism or other substance abuse.
  False. Although the two often go together, many substance abusers never offend, and many offenders do not use alcohol or other drugs.
- Incest is less harmful than rape or sexual abuse from strangers.
  False. Incest can be even more damaging because it is a severe betrayal by the very people the child needs to depend on, and there is often no escape from the abuser.
- Children and adolescents become victims due to their own seductive behavior.
  False. While children and adolescents may become seductive or even promiscuous, this happens because they have been victims of sexual abuse, usually from an adult.

What are some of your beliefs about offenders? _____

_____

_____

_____

_____

_____

_____

_____

_____

Perpetrators abuse for different reasons and in different ways. There are certain preconditions for the abuse to occur:

- Access to the child. If offenders don't have access, they can't abuse. They are creative in finding children if there are none at home. Sometimes they marry women with children; sometimes they get jobs around children. More children are, in fact, abused by people known to them than by strangers.
- Rationalization of offending behavior. Although most abusers know this behavior is against the law, they find ways to tell themselves that what they are doing is okay. They may use drugs or alcohol and blame the substance for their behavior. Sometimes offenders rationalize that they are providing sex education for the children. They often convince themselves and their victims that the victims were responsible.
- Confidence of not getting caught. Usually offenders abuse when they are alone with their victims. They may use threats to keep the victims quiet. If the abuse is known to others, it continues because the perpetrators are in positions of power over those people and feel confident of not being stopped.

Some offenders prefer boys, some prefer girls, and others abuse both. Alan would abuse any child, even his own children, Joseph, 5, and Janine, 3, while they were visiting him after their parents' divorce. The abuse continued for a year before their mother took them to the doctor because of genital infections. The doctor determined that both children had been sexually abused, and all visits with their father were stopped. Alan is an example of a child molester who will molest any young child regardless of sex or age. Although he had been married, his primary sexual interest was toward children. He was unable to maintain an intimate adult relationship for any length of time.

There are offenders who abuse only when they are stressed or depressed or drunk. Some offenders abuse children or adolescents of a particular age. James began offending at age 11 after he had been abused. As he got older, he continued to abuse when he became stressed. He abused only 11-year-old girls.

Some offenders abuse children of all ages. They are usually good at hiding their acts, and frequently they are respected members of the community. They are often masters at manipulation and will continue to abuse children until they are stopped. Henry abused his daughter from an early age until she left home to get married. Many years later when a child accused Henry of molesting her, it came out that he had been abusing his grandchildren as well as neighbors' children. When confronted, he rationalized his behavior and told police that the children had been seductive with him. Many perpetrators rationalize to convince themselves they aren't doing anything wrong.

There are offenders who act violently and are aroused by the feeling of power that violence gives them. These offenders are *sociopaths:* people who have no consciences and feel neither guilt nor remorse for the harm they do. They are concerned only with getting their own needs met.

Other offenders dissociate when they abuse. These offenders are likely to have had particularly severe histories of having been sexually or physically abused themselves.

Many offenders were themselves abused, but this does not mean that everyone who has been abused will abuse others. Many victims never abuse. Sexual abuse of children by adults is sometimes seen as addictive behavior, but choice is always involved, and the abuser is always accountable for his or her actions.

Sexual behaviors develop over time, beginning in childhood. Young children of similar ages often play "doctor"—both, as willing participants, examining each other's bodies. This game is usually harmless as long as there is no forced activity. Exploration of this type is, in fact, one of the ways we learn about our bodies.

Young children who have been abused often act out sexually. They may expose themselves, touch each other's genitals, or make sexual comments inappropriate for their ages. This behavior, referred to as *aggravated sexual play,* is different from normal play, but these young children are not considered offenders.

Many perpetrators begin abusing while they are in their teens or even younger. They are considered juvenile offenders. There are different reasons that adolescents abuse, including the following general ones:

- The adolescents were abused themselves and take their feelings out on younger children.
- Some adolescents are socially immature. They are uncomfortable with others their age, don't have many peer relationships, and find it easier to relate to younger children who can be taken advantage of and who will look up to them.
- Some adolescents who have no access to other teens for sexual exploration use younger children to learn about sex.

Adolescents who accept responsibility for abusing can be helped by juvenile offender groups and by individual therapy.

Treatment is more difficult if the offender is an adult and has been abusing for a long time, if he or she has become addicted to the sexual behavior or to the excitement and danger involved, and if he or she has built up years of denial and rationalization.

Sexual abuse may be a one-time event, or it may continue for years. The majority of cases involve someone the child knows. It is usually an ongoing relationship in which the abuse begins subtly and progresses to overt sexual behavior.

About Your Own Experience

What do you already know about abuser(s)? _____

_____

_____

_____

Who was (were) your abuser(s)? _____

_____

_____

_____

How did your abuser(s) approach you? _____

_____

_____

_____

Where were you abused? _____

_____

_____

_____

What do you think made the abuse possible? _____

_____

_____

_____

_____

How long did the abuse continue? _____

_____

_____

_____

_____

Did you blame yourself? _____ *How?* _____

_____

_____

_____

_____

_____

_____

_____

_____

What do you think about your abuser? _____

_____

_____

_____

_____

_____

_____

Is there anything you would do differently now? _____ *What?*__

_____

_____

_____

_____

_____

_____

_____

Did your abuser resemble any of the perpetrators we discussed?

_____ *If yes, how? If no, how was yours different?* _____

_____

_____

_____

_____

_____

_____

Do you have any other thoughts? _____

_____

_____

_____

_____

_____

_____

_____

_____

_____

9

Sexuality and Sexual Abuse

This chapter discusses sexuality and how it develops. It will help you determine the effect of abuse on your sexuality and what you can do about it.

The term *sexuality* refers to several aspects of your sexual identity and experience. First, sexuality concerns how you feel about your body. Learning to like and care about your body is important to your healthy sexual adjustment. Developing a good sexual relationship does involve intimacy and good feelings about the other person, but it's important to have good feelings about yourself and your own body first. If you dislike your body, it's hard to share it with someone else.

Children first learn about their bodies by touching themselves and each other. When touching feels good, it may lead to masturbation—stimulating oneself sexually. Many people masturbate both before and during their sexually active years. Some religions and families discourage it, and there are myths linking masturbation with such problems as sterility, blindness, or insanity. These are *definitely myths*. Masturbation is harmful only when it is used in an uncontrollable way to avoid being with friends or to avoid feelings. Otherwise, it's a normal and harmless activity.

We are all born sexual beings; we all have the potential for sexual interest and sexual responses. For example, baby boys get erections. There are a number of causes, including having their diapers changed. Over time we learn, and naturally develop, responses to seeing sexy pictures, reading romantic or sexual books, or seeing an attractive boy or girl. This means our sexuality is developing, and we react not only to physical stimulation but also to emotional triggers.

Sometime before the age of 5, we develop a gender identity. We know what sex we are, and we are becoming aware of the social roles considered "appropriate" to our sex. We receive reinforcement from family and friends who model feminine and masculine ways. Girls are usually encouraged to play quietly with dolls, while boys are encouraged to play with toy trucks and planes. Sex roles are changing, though, and the pressure is lessening for girls and boys to behave differently.

Parents and society teach children about sex indirectly by the ways they communicate values and taboos about the body, as you can observe for yourself by thinking about the words commonly used for the genital areas. For example, the term *privates* signifies something to be hidden.

Having a good self-image and accepting yourself as a sexual being are important factors in your developing sexuality. Many teenagers have problems with both. Adolescence is a time of sexual awakening. While sexual fantasies are normal for people of all ages, adolescence brings an increase in both fantasies and sexual awareness. Such dreams and fantasies may lead to feelings of shame; nevertheless, they simply signify that sexuality is developing normally.

Peer pressure about sexual issues during adolescence is common. Many teenagers believe they have to be sexually active in order to be accepted and to be "normal." Many get involved in sexual relationships before they are ready emotionally. Before you take this step, you should see yourself as a worthy person, apart from how much others like you. Having an older person with whom you can comfortably discuss sexual issues can help you sort out these feelings.

We learn sexual attitudes in a variety of ways, and many of the messages clash with one another. "Sex is good." "Sex is bad." "Boys are only after one thing." "Girls can't be trusted; they will use you."

What other conflicting statements about sex have you heard?

_____

_____

_____

_____

_____

_____

_____

Most commonly, sexual relationships are heterosexual, meaning relationships and sexual acts between members of opposite sexes. This is the most widely accepted form of sexual expression. Some people are homosexual; they are involved in relationships and sexual acts with members of the same sex. No one knows what makes a person heterosexual or homosexual. Either sort of relationship can be healthy and fulfilling.

The desire to experience one's sexuality is strong and helps a person to overcome the conflicting messages about sex. In healthy relationships, couples work at overcoming any distrust they may have learned. They can become friends as well as lovers. They can learn to accept and enjoy their own bodies as well as each other's. They can enjoy their differences. They can experience affection as well as sexual desire. They can trust that neither wants to hurt the other. Lovers can touch each other physically with affection that does not necessarily lead to sex. They can also enjoy an active sex life. There is a physical expression of affection before, during, and after sexual relations.

If you've been sexually abused, you may have trouble developing a healthy sexual identity. You may feel bad about yourself and your body and have difficulty being intimate with and trusting others.

At times you may have responded physically when you didn't want to. You may have hated what was happening or been ashamed or frightened. You could have been very angry at the offender, yet your body may have responded, and you may today experience feelings of arousal with someone who is rough or sadistic. The clitoris and penis are very sensitive to sexual stimulation; touch there can cause a sexual response, including orgasm. For boys, the state of arousal, an erection, is obvious, leading to extreme feelings of shame. For girls the physical response, while less visible, still causes shame.

You don't want to say that it did arouse you. It's absolutely the most embarrassing thing. You feel totally wrong for saying it. And that you can't blame it on the abuser if you like it. It's guilt I guess. It's just embarrassing. I don't think I've ever mentioned it to anybody until right now. I've never said one thing about it 'cause it's like a big, dark secret. That's kind of the one last thing that I've never ever said to anybody. I didn't want to admit it to myself, let alone tell anybody that. (Erin, 17)

When children experience pleasurable feelings during the abuse, they may later feel awful. Sometimes the only love and attention children get is during the sexual abuse. Therefore, they may look forward to the abuse in order to get the nurturing. Then they think it must be their fault because they "liked it" or "wanted it." If you have ever felt this way, it is important for you to know that **children do *not* cause abuse to happen to them.** Sexual abuse is a violation of boundaries and of personal space. It doesn't have to be painful to be abuse. The responsibility always belongs to the offender. He or she chose to abuse you. Even if you liked it, looked forward to it, and thought you set up situations for it to happen, **the responsibility belongs to the offender.**

Have you ever felt this way? _____

_____

_____

_____

_____

_____

Children who have been abused sometimes act seductively because such behavior is often rewarded during abuse. Responsible adults never use this as an excuse to act sexually with children. A responsible adult is concerned and tries to find out why the child is being seductive.

As a result of their abuse, some teenagers become hypersexual, or unusually or excessively active or concerned about sexual matters. They may be trying:

To get attention.

To prove that they're not homosexual or to prove that homosexuality is okay if they are gay.

To master a fear of sex.

To make sure all their "parts" work.

To experience a good feeling.

To gain a sense of power and control.

If you are frequently sexual, what are your reasons? _____

_____

_____

_____

_____

_____

Hypersexual behavior can change when you explore and interpret the effects of having been abused. Talking with a therapist about these issues may be difficult but ultimately helpful. While you may feel ashamed at first, talking will help you to understand what happened, and it will also help to take some of the shame away.

The rest of this chapter concerns specific aspects of sexual behavior. We are not encouraging or even condoning sexual activity for you. We believe there are many issues to think about before becoming sexually active. The decision is best made after you have educated yourself about the physical and emotional consequences. You should consider the risks involved, such as venereal disease, AIDS, and pregnancy. Furthermore, having sex before you're ready can cause you increased feelings of worthlessness and shame. Although we encourage you to wait and make this decision in a thoughtful way, we know that many teenagers do have sex. If you are one of them, this next section is for you.

If You Are Having Sex Now

No matter how you reacted to abuse at the time, it may be affecting you now in ways you aren't aware of. You may not realize that it could be causing present problems. Some teens we know who were tortured have told us that they can be sexually aroused only when their partner is rough or frightening. Others say they can't get turned on unless the situation is the same as it was during the abuse. Some get aroused by thinking about the abuse while they masturbate. Still others say they shut down, space out, leave their bodies, or panic when they participate in sex or any other activity that reminds them of their abuse.

You may have negative reactions to certain sexual or even nonsexual situations that remind you of what happened long ago. For example, a number of girls tell us they hate having anyone touch their faces, especially their jaws. All of them were forced to have oral sex, and the offenders held the girls' heads and jaws. Mary can't eat certain kinds of candy that reminded her of her abuse. Beth couldn't eat ice cream cones because it reminded her of details of the oral sex she was forced into.

> He would take my head and make me have oral sex. Even to this day I can't have anything in my mouth, like my keychain, plastic stuff . . . (Sarah, 19)

Sometimes sexual activities cause flashbacks or anxiety, even if you have no memory of the actual abuse. The body as well as the mind holds memories. Doing something similar now can automatically cause a memory to come close to the surface from "nowhere" or trigger the same fear you felt during the abuse.

> I'd see people, and if they even kissed me, I'd freak out and I'd break up with them, even if I liked them a lot. The first time a kid kissed me, I fell asleep in the middle of it. And then the first time a guy went up my shirt, I puked. When someone was kissing me or something, I'd feel totally helpless, like I had no voice. If they were doing something I didn't want them to do, I wouldn't say no 'cause I had no voice and it's like I couldn't talk. That was the worst part of all—just feeling like a Gumby doll and not having any control over myself or anything. (Paula, 19)

Sandy, 18 years old, said that at times while having sex, everything would go dark and she would feel like a little girl. She wouldn't know where she was or who she was with. Sixteen-year-old Carol said that if her boyfriend touched her a certain way, she would see her father's face instead of her boyfriend's. When this happened, she felt scared but was too embarrassed to tell him. She pretended nothing was wrong, but she felt like a frightened little girl.

For many people who are uncomfortable with sex, being in complete control of the situation has made them better able to have and even enjoy sex. Being in control for them means initiating sex, deciding what will happen, and when to end it. Some get this control in a healthy way by talking with their partners about their needs. Others, to control their fears, control the situation by being sexually promiscuous—having sex with many different partners. They believe if they "choose" to have sex, then they are in control. Some girls think that sex is all they are "good for"; they have received this message from an early age. Some boys feel they have to "perform" sexually and be "studs" even if they're not ready to be sexual. Because of this, boys sometimes think there is something wrong with them, and they make up stories of sexual conquests to hide their fears. Boys shouldn't have to be "studs" any more than girls should have to be sexual objects in order to be liked and accepted.

Some teenagers feel uncomfortable, terrified, or damaged when they engage in any sexual touching. Others feel loved, appreciated, worthwhile, and needed. Many have a mix of feelings. It's important to pay attention to your reactions to sexual situations now.

How do you feel before, during, and after sexual behavior? Make a list, analyzing how you feel about different situations, such as hand holding, kissing, petting, and intercourse.

Before [situation] _____.

I feel _____.

Afterward I feel _____.

Before [situation] _____.

I feel _____.

Afterward I feel _____.

Before [situation] _____.

I feel _____.

Afterward I feel _____.

Before [situation] _____.

I feel _____.

Afterward I feel _____.

If you feel bad before, during, or after sexual activity, stop the activity for now. Talk with someone who can help you to sort out your feelings, and teach you how to take better care of yourself.

The first step toward developing a healthy sexual relationship is to respect yourself. You do this by learning to know, accept, and like yourself. Next, it's important to know how to have friendships with people of either sex. Friendship involves intimacy and trust, as well as give and take. It may take a long time to heal sexually and undo damage from the past. While this may seem impossible at times, we know many survivors who, with courage, patience, and therapy, have gone on to develop rewarding relationships, both sexual and nonsexual.

PART II

Healing

10

From Surviving to Thriving

I n this chapter we discuss healing from sexual abuse. Although we describe the stages in a certain order, people don't necessarily heal in an organized way. You may see yourself going through the "stages" differently, or going back and forth from one to another. There is no right or wrong way to recover. By reading this book, you're already taking a big step along the way.

1. Accept that there is a problem. This is the first step in solving any problem, and so it is with sexual abuse. Admitting that there is a problem can cause a lot of pain, and trying to avoid pain is natural.

You may not have remembered the abuse for a long time; you may have remembered the abuse but believed that it didn't cause any problems; or you may think that dwelling on the past is what actually creates the problems.

What do you believe? _____

_____

_____

_____

_____

Once you've accepted that the abuse happened and that it did create problems, you can begin to recover.

2. Keep yourself safe during the healing process. Staying safe doesn't mean having no pain; healing is painful. We strongly advise you to get the help of a good therapist. Also develop a support system of people you can trust, and use it. Talk with the people on your safety list about when and why you might need to call them, and call them when you need to.

3. Remember the details of the abuse. This is often a difficult step. Many survivors find significant chunks of memory missing. Working on healing often brings up these memories. A trained therapist can help you to remember. Restoring the missing chunks of your life helps you to deal with the pain.

4. Share the experience of your abuse with another person. This step is vital to the healing process. There are two totally different kinds of sharing, and both are helpful. One is sharing the details with a trained therapist. This person helps you to put the abuse into a perspective you can live with—taking it out of the dark and ridding it of the secrecy that allowed the abuse to happen and continue. This helps you to put the blame where it belongs. It helps you to take back the power that was stolen from you.

The second kind of sharing involves telling other people who are supportive of you. In this kind, you don't have to go into the details. You can choose what to tell, and you can choose who to tell: a friend, a counselor, a doctor, your parents, or anyone else of your choice.

5. Develop good self-esteem. Once you've taken the secrets out of hiding, you can look at them more objectively and realistically and begin to see the abuse as it really was. You can learn to stop blaming yourself and let go of the shame and guilt. Then you will want more out of life. You can learn to treat yourself better. You can, with your therapist's help, begin to rebuild your self esteem.

6. Develop healthy relationships. You may not know how and where to begin, but you can learn. (Building self-esteem and developing healthy relationships will be dealt with more fully in the following chapters.)

A final empowering step in your healing might be to confront your offender. Some offenders, however, are dangerous, and there are different ways to deal with this. Chapter 15 explains confrontation more completely.

Once you have reached this point in your healing, you will probably want to have more fun in your life. There is a chapter on this too. We hope you continue the good work you've begun.

11

Remembering and Sharing the Story of Your Abuse

C hildhood sexual abuse can be so traumatic that many survivors dissociate from and block out all memory of it. Some forget certain incidents but remember others. Many remember factual details but not the feelings. Each person has a unique way of dissociating from memories of abuse and of remembering later. No particular way is right or wrong. Dissociating is simply a way of surviving trauma.

While reading this book, you may have begun to reexperience old feelings or memories. This is natural. Knowing about others' experiences often brings back your own. Keep a journal of the memories so that you have them available when you want and not have to think about them all the time. Talk with your therapist about this and about other options for dealing with memories.

You may be asking yourself, "Why would I want to remember things that were so terrible and scary? I would prefer to forget that this stuff ever happened to me." Memories are important because they help you to gain perspective about the past abuse and help you to understand the abuse. What you thought and felt during the abuse has a lot to do with how you think and feel today. For example, if you felt frightened and ashamed about what was being done to you, you probably still feel frightened and ashamed today. Whether you consciously think about the abuse or not, if you felt it was your fault at the time, you probably feel that things happening now are also your fault.

Dealing with memories and feelings is important to your healing; otherwise, they complicate your life. You may feel anxious and not know why. Little frustrations may trigger rage. You may have trouble with close relationships. You may sometimes feel badly about yourself. And the memories will not go away until you acknowledge and deal with them.

Working through the pain of the abuse is a process. First, you admit to yourself that the abuse happened. Then you learn how to handle feelings, including those about day-to-day issues as well as those from the past.

Before you continue with this chapter, talk with your therapist about how you will take care of yourself if or when you begin to get overwhelmed. Some ways might be to pamper yourself with a treat or use relaxation or talk with a trusted friend or family member. Practice the techniques you and your therapist think will help. Then, before you deal with memories, practice taking care of yourself in day to day stressful situations. Use your list of safe people if you want to talk. Will you be able to reach your therapist between appointments if you need to? Do you know how to do relaxation when you feel stressed out? Get these support systems set up *before* you begin the memory work.

Once you've been able to gain some confidence in managing overwhelming feelings, the next step in therapy is to remember and share the details of the abuse. Decide with your therapist when you are ready for this.

Most people feel extremely ashamed of what happened and of their part in it. They think they could never tell anyone about it, fearing that the other person will reject them or be repulsed by them. Sharing the details of your story with someone who cares, however, will help take the shame away. It will allow you to experience a positive, caring response from another human being—something you probably didn't get while the abuse was going on. Sharing the details means talking about the *entire* experience: where the abuse happened, what your offender did, what he or she made you do, how you felt, and what you thought.

Sharing is particularly difficult because you will reexperience many of the feelings you experienced during the abuse. *We strongly advise you to do this work with your therapist.*

When you're ready to tell your story, plan it out with your therapist. Tell him or her what you need.

- Will you need a special session, or can it be during your regular therapy time?
- Will you need a longer session, or will you need time at the end to relax and pull yourself together?
- How do you want your therapist to respond while you share?
- Will you want something to hold—a stuffed animal or a blanket?
- Do you want to draw pictures to express some of your feelings?

Think about these things, discuss them, and plan the session or sessions so that you get your needs met.

12

To Tell or Not to Tell

Breaking the Silence About Sexual Abuse

This chapter is about telling people other than your therapist that you were abused. That *doesn't* mean sharing your complete story, as in therapy. It means letting some other people know in general terms what happened to you.

Breaking the silence about sexual abuse can be a powerful tool for healing, but it can also cause some serious problems for you. This chapter will explain how telling can help, and help you decide whether disclosing is right for you now.

The reasons for disclosing abuse are different for each person and for each situation. Sharing this information generally helps to dissolve the shame associated with the secret. Most survivors think they had to keep the abuse a secret: they could be blamed for what happened; they could get into trouble; they wouldn't be believed. These feelings all contribute to the survivor's sense of shame and guilt for what happened. You were probably told—verbally or otherwise—to keep what was happening a secret between you and your perpetrator or within the family. Therefore, you were likely to experience negative feelings about yourself. Telling can be a powerful way of removing the blame and shame from you and putting it back where it belongs: on the person who abused you.

The two most common reasons that victims disclose their abuse are to find help and support for the pain they are in and to get help in stopping the abuse if it is still going on. Other important reasons include the following:*

---

*Christine A. Courtois, *Healing the Incest Wound: Adult Survivors in Therapy* (New York: W. W. Norton & Co., 1988), p. 328.

Decreasing their shame.

Validating that their experiences were terrible and frightening.

Getting support.

Getting relief from guilt.

Feeling less isolated.

Preventing the offender from abusing others.

Expressing anger.

Getting revenge.

Taking back personal power.

Every person has his or her own reasons for deciding to disclose.

What are yours? _____

_____

_____

_____

_____

_____

_____

Once you decide to tell, the next question is: Who will you tell? Telling for the first time takes the most courage. It means you are asking for help, either in making the situation stop or in working through the pain and after-effects. It also indicates that you are beginning to take care of yourself. You are ready to take back your power.

If you have already shared this information and you're now deciding to disclose to others, you're making a further conscious decision to let go of the pain and shame. Decide who else to tell, when, and for what reasons.

Initially choose people who will be most supportive. Being careful about who you tell and why is a way of protecting and taking care of yourself. Think about the people in your life who support you (refer to the list you made). Which of these people do you think will stand by you if you tell them about the abuse? How do you think they will respond? How do you want them to respond? Make a list.

Name	Expected response	Desired response
_____	_____	_____
_____	_____	_____
_____	_____	_____
_____	_____	_____
_____	_____	_____
_____	_____	_____
_____	_____	_____

Now think about each of these people. How would it help you if he or she knew about the abuse? For example, if you tell your best friends, would they be more understanding of your mood swings? Would it help you to share more of your feelings in general? If you tell your brother, would he stop hanging around with the person who abused you? If you tell your mother and father, would they stop the abuse and protect you from the perpetrator and/or remove that person from the house? If you tell your counselor, would he or she help you to work through your feelings and help you to get protection? Think about what you need from each of these people, and ask yourself whether telling them about the abuse could help you to get it.

I want to tell _____, *because I need*

him (her) to _____

_____

_____

I want to tell _____, *because I need*

him (her) to _____

_____

_____

I want to tell _____, *because I need*

him (her) to _____

_____

_____

After you've thought about the benefits of telling, think about the risks. Will your family be angry? Will friends tell others without your permission? Will anyone think differently of you? If you tell an adult, will that adult take advantage of you? What could you lose if you tell?

What are some of the risks involved in telling? _____

_____

_____

_____

_____

Now that you've thought of both the benefits and the risks if disclosing seems right for you, pick one person. Decide on a time and place to tell that person and on exactly what you want him or her to know. Do you want your friend to know only that you were sexually abused or also who the perpetrator was? Do you want to tell him or her at what age(s) you were abused? Do you want to go into specifics about what happened. Which facts do you want your friend to keep confidential? He or she may ask you questions such as, "Who did it?" or, "How old were you?" or "Why didn't you tell me before?" (a parent will often ask this). You need to be prepared for these questions so that you share only what feels right and comfortable for you. Decide who, when and where you will tell, and what you want to tell for now:

I will tell _____. *It will be on* _____

_____ *at* _____

I want him (her) to know _____

_____

_____

_____

_____ *because I need him (her) to* _____

_____

_____

_____

I am not going to tell him (her) _____

_____

_____

_____

If I'm asked questions I'm not comfortable answering, I will say:

_____

_____

_____

People in certain positions, such as teachers and counselors, are required by law to report information about abuse to the child welfare authorities, especially if the abuse was by a family member who still lives with you. When you disclose to any of them, you are asking them to help you. Discuss the safest way for them to help, and ask that they keep you aware of whatever action they take. If the abuse has already come out and the appropriate actions have already been taken, they may not have to make such a report.

If you are disclosing about a close family member, the news may be shocking to others in your family, and they could respond with disbelief or even anger. It might be useful to ask your counselor to help you disclose to your family. While many families eventually adjust to such news, some families deny it, become angry, and blame the victim. Although this reaction is extremely painful, an incest situation is far more damaging and it must not be allowed to continue. Sarah's mother didn't believe her:

> After the incident with my sister seeing, my sister told my mother what she saw. My mother talked to me the next morning about it and I said, "Yes, it is true." She basically asked me if I was having sex with her husband. I said, "No, he is having sex with me. I'm not doing anything." Basically I had no idea what the word even meant. My mother called him up; he came home; he denied it. I was up in my room hiding, literally hiding. I locked the bedroom door and hid in my closet. My mother called me downstairs, and she called me a liar, slapped me, and sent me to school, and said she never wanted to hear such a lie again. I was mad that she didn't believe me because my sister had seen it. (Sarah, 19)

Another possibility when you tell your parents or others who love you is that they may have strong reactions on your behalf. They may become angry at the abuser, cry, feel guilty, become overprotective, worry about you more, constantly ask if you are all right, and generally seem different for a time. This is not unusual. Eventually your parents will adjust to the news, and life at home will settle down.

> In school, we were writing papers, and I picked abuse to do my paper on. And then I just told my teacher, and then she kind of backed me into a corner. It was, "Either you tell your parents, or I'll tell them." And I knew that, going into it, but I think knowing that I had no choice was so much easier. She made me. I knew going into it that she was going to make me do that. I mean, I think legally she has to. So, I told my mom that night. At first, she was like, "Well, what do you

mean?" when I said he abused me—just in case my idea of it was much different from her, you know. When I told her, she lost it. She really lost it. I've never seen my mother like that, ever. I mean, she cried when we moved, but it wasn't like hysterical bawling. I mean, she lost it. And then my father came in while she was crying. She made him promise not to do anything. My poor father thought someone had died. And she told him, and he was okay. He was like, "Oh, my God!" He just sat down. But that was tough. All those years [the perpetrator] had told me that everyone was going to be upset if I told, you know. And then I told, and they were upset. (Amber, 17)

Although strong reactions may happen, tell anyway! If you are in therapy, ask your therapist to help you prepare to disclose to your parents or to any other person you want to tell. You may decide to have your parents come to a session with your therapist and tell your story there so that you will have extra support.

It may be easier to tell someone outside your family—a friend, boyfriend, girlfriend, or teacher—because you don't share with this person the emotional ties that you have with your parents. The disclosure still may be difficult, but you probably won't have to prepare for the intensity of reaction that you might expect from your family. Regardless of whom you're telling, plan carefully so that you get what you need.

You are choosing to tell so that *you* can heal from the abuse. Take your time, think about what you need, plan thoughtfully what you want to say, and ask for help to make this process easier and more useful for you.

Developing Self-Esteem

You're now at a point in healing to evaluate yourself. This means examining your sense of self, your self-esteem. Only when you have healthy self-esteem can you develop good, satisfying relationships with others.

Healing means seeing yourself as more than a victim of abuse. It means recognizing your talents, strengths, and individuality and appreciating and liking yourself as the unique individual you are.

Healing involves learning to relate to others in healthy, honest, and respectful ways and expecting the same in return. It means knowing when you're not getting your needs met and doing something about it. Both tasks—developing good self-esteem and developing healthy relationships—are difficult.

If the important people in your life gave you the message that you were worthless, you most likely believed them. If you still believe it, you probably aren't taking good care of yourself now and don't expect others to take care of your either. Learning to like, respect and care for yourself takes time and work. These attitude changes deserve close attention.

Self-Esteem

"To esteem" means to respect or value something. Self-esteem means feeling respectful toward yourself. Respecting yourself and believing you have value does not make you conceited, and it doesn't mean that you think of yourself as better than others. It's about how you feel toward yourself, not how you feel about others.

People with good self-esteem don't necessarily like everything about themselves—they may think they need to lose weight or do better in school—but they have a general feeling of self-worth. People who have low or no self-esteem believe they aren't as important or as valuable as others. They don't expect people to treat them with respect because they don't respect themselves. When others treat them badly, they make excuses or brush it off as unimportant. People with low self-esteem may put others' needs and feelings before their own, sometimes without even realizing what they are doing. They often feel badly and don't realize it's because they haven't paid attention to their own needs. Does any of this sound like you? If it does, the following exercises on improving your self-esteem will give you ways to begin changing.

Begin by looking at how you feel about yourself today. This means thinking about your total self, your body, your personality, your intelligence, and your behavior.

My name is _____. *If I were to pick a new name it would be* _____. *I (like, don't like) my actual name because* _____.

I am _____ *tall and weigh* _____ *pounds. Generally, when I look in the mirror I feel* _____.

My best feature is my _____; *my worst feature is my* _____. *I would describe my personality as (outgoing, shy, friendly, boring, aggressive, domineering, easy going)* (Pick one or use your own description).

_____

_____

_____

The features of my personality that I like are _____

_____

_____

_____

The aspects of my personality that I would like to change are

_____

_____

_____

Write a description of the way you usually feel about yourself.

_____

_____

_____

Are your answers generally positive or negative? Did you know you felt this way about yourself? Most people don't spend much time thinking about how they feel about themselves. But when something bad happens, they blame themselves and think less of themselves. Yet when something good happens, they don't give themselves credit.

Thinking about your feelings will help you to decide which of them you want to change and which are fine just as they are. This will ultimately help you to feel better about yourself. For example, if you feel bad because people seem to use you—sexually, for money or favors—you can take better care of yourself by saying no. You don't always have to do what other people want you to do. In time, you will feel better by standing up for yourself, and you will have more self-respect. You will like yourself more, and take even better care of yourself.

Another way to improve self-esteem is to change your self-concept. Try this exercise: Make a short list of a few negative thoughts and feelings you have about yourself. Use only the left column for this part. Keep your list to the space provided. The idea is for you to practice changing attitudes you have about yourself. Now consider ways to change those old thoughts and feelings. For each issue raised in the left column, write a related positive statement on the right. For example, to the right of "I hate my body," you might write, "I'm very modest about my body." For "I always say stupid things," you could put, "I'm too honest, and people don't always like what I say." Make a new statement for each negative you wrote. If you have trouble, ask one of your support people to help you. This exercise will take time, so even if you don't feel better right away, keep working at it. Your feelings will change.

Negatives about myself	Positive reframe

Next, make a list of your positive qualities, strengths, skills, and talents. List the things you are proud of and that others compliment you on. For example, if you got a B in a subject that you have done poorly in previously, list that. If you were told you are a good tennis player, put that down. If your friends told you that your hair is gorgeous, that counts too. Even if you don't believe your friends or think these qualities aren't significant, put them on the list anyway. Until you feel good about yourself, you probably won't give yourself much credit.

Things I like about myself or that others think are special

_____   _____

_____   _____

_____   _____

_____   _____

_____   _____

_____   _____

_____   _____

_____   _____

_____   _____

_____   _____

We made this list long because there are undoubtedly many positive points about you, even if *you* don't know it yet. You may think of only one or two things at first. Don't let this bother you. If you can't fill this list now, come back to it as you realize more good things about yourself. If you can fill it all in now, great! Use more paper if you need to. Add to it often, and think about your special qualities every day. This doesn't mean you are conceited or selfish; it just means that you are learning to appreciate who you are. If you're worried about what others would say if they knew about your list, don't tell them. Remember, you are doing this to take care of yourself, not to impress others.

Having good self-esteem means:

- You will take care of yourself.
- You will pay attention to your feelings and needs.
- You won't let yourself regularly get exhausted or go hungry.

- You won't put yourself in abusive situations.
- You won't hang out with people who hurt your feelings.
- You will be able to trust your instincts and keep out of danger.

What do you now do to take care of yourself? _____

_____

_____

_____

_____

What could you do to take better care of yourself? _____

_____

_____

_____

_____

Forgiving Yourself for Mistakes

A part of healing your whole self is forgiving yourself for the mistakes you make now and for what you did to survive during the abuse. Many survivors are hard on themselves; they get angry and beat themselves up emotionally for even small mistakes. Although we talked about attitudes toward mistakes in chapter 4 on families, we want you to think about them again.

How do you feel about yourself when you behave less than perfectly in a situation? Can you let it go, or do you worry about what happened and what others think about you? Are you able to say, "Oh well, I learned something, and I'll do better next time"? Can you still like yourself, or do you end up hating yourself?

All of us make mistakes; no one is perfect. Making mistakes is not an indication of your worth as a person; it doesn't make you good or bad. Learn how to be gentle with yourself. Separate who you are from the mistakes you make. This may be new and difficult for you, but it is well worth doing. Try this exercise:

Write about a mistake you made recently. _____

_____

_____

_____

_____

_____

How did you feel about yourself after? _____

_____

_____

_____

_____

If your best friend made the same mistake, what advice would you give to him or her? _____

_____

_____

_____

_____

How would you feel about that friend? _____

_____

_____

_____

Now close your eyes and imagine yourself as your own best friend. Repeat the advice you just gave your friend, but this time, give it to yourself. Imagine forgiving yourself as you would forgive someone else. If you have a hard time with forgiving yourself, talk with your therapist or another supportive person. Forgiving yourself is a huge issue in itself. We will delve into it in chapter 16.

Talk with your therapist about behaviors you want to change.

Things I wish I hadn't done recently: _____

_____

_____

_____

_____

_____

_____

To begin developing better self-esteem, share the reasons you feel ashamed or worthless; listen to and believe people who value you; recognize your talents and accomplishments; forgive your mistakes. This will take time and hard work. Be patient, and you'll find that your attitude about yourself can change.

14

Developing Healthy Relationships

One goal in healing is to have healthy relationships. By "healthy," we mean a relationship in which each person feels valued, respected, and listened to. There is open communication; friends and family can talk about their thoughts and feelings. If you don't like something that others do, you can tell them without fear of their turning on you. You believe that they don't want to hurt you, and they know you wouldn't try to hurt them. In healthy relationships, each makes compromises. No one **always** gives in or feels abused, frightened, or put down. Healthy relationships are satisfying. All get their needs met much of the time. While there are trade-offs, people need not sacrifice themselves.

It's difficult to develop healthy relationships if you don't feel good about yourself. People with low self-esteem tend to let others use them and take them for granted. They seldom stand up for themselves for fear of offending others or being called selfish. They may eventually blow up over something minor because they've let resentments build up.

If you have low self-esteem, you could be giving to others, not expecting them to give in return. You may be criticized but not defend yourself at the time. Later you may overreact to something minor. Maybe you do things that others want you to but feel uncomfortable.

Your feelings are important. You must take care of yourself; otherwise you may behave in ways you don't like. One way to begin caring for yourself is to notice how you behave with others and how you allow them to treat you. Following are some questions, divided into two parts, because you might behave quite differently with friends than you do with family, or you may be surprised at the similarities. After you finish this exercise, talk with your therapist or someone else you trust about your answers and your reactions to them.

I usually help out a friend in need, but I rarely ask for help when I need it. Yes ___ No ___ *Why?* _____

_____

_____

_____

_____

I usually help a family member in need, but I rarely ask for help when I need it. Yes ___ No ___ *Why?* _____

_____

_____

_____

_____

When my friends disappoint me, I usually (tell them, keep it to myself, rationalize their behavior) (circle one) because _____

_____

_____

When my family dissappoints me, I usually (tell them, keep it to myself, rationalize their behavior) (circle one) because _____

_____

_____

_____

When I am angry at friends, I usually (tell them, keep it to myself, make excuses for their behavior, or _____

because _____

_____

When I am angry at family members I usually (tell them, keep it to myself, make excuses for their behavior, or _____

because _____

_____

When a friend is angry at me I feel _____

_____

When a family member is angry at me I feel _____

_____

I will usually react to a friend's anger by _____

_____

I will usually react to a family member's anger by _____

_____

When friends do something nice for me, I usually feel (circle all that apply): *surprised, happy, touched, guilty, vulnerable, suspicious, indebted to them, other* _____

_____

When family members do something nice for me, I usually feel (circle all that apply): *surprised, happy, touched, guilty, vulnerable, suspicious, indebted to them, other* _____

_____

When I do something nice for a friend, I expect him or her to

_____

*When I do something nice for a family member, I expect him or her
to* _____

_____

I think my friends see me as someone who _____

_____

I think my family sees me as someone who _____

_____

Are you surprised by any of your answers? Perhaps you can think
of situations in which you would like to behave differently or situations in which you would like to be treated differently. Write down
how you would like things to change and what you can do to
achieve this change. Be specific.

I want the following to be different with my friends: _____

_____

_____

_____

_____

I can change my part in the situation by _____

_____

_____

_____

_____

I want the following to be different with my family: _____

_____

_____

_____

_____

_____

_____

I can change my part in the situation by _____

_____

_____

_____

_____

It takes time and work to change the way you relate to others and the way they relate to you. You won't be able to do it overnight, so don't be disappointed if you don't see results immediately. Keep at it. Notice your behavior in relationships and the ways that others behave toward you. Be aware of what feels good and what doesn't.

Begin by making small changes. For example, if your friend is always late when you've made plans, tell him or her, in a nice but clear way, that this bothers you. If your brother talks to you only when he wants to borrow money, let him know this annoys you. Make a list of things you want to change in your relationships and what you want to say to the other person. This will teach you to communicate your feelings and needs.

In my relationship with _____, *I don't*

like _____

_____

_____

_____

This is what I will say or do about it: _____

_____

_____

_____

In my relationship with _____, *I don't*

like _____

_____

_____

This is what I will say or do about it: _____

_____

_____

_____

In my relationship with _____. *I don't*

like _____

_____

_____

This is what I will say or do about it: _____

_____

_____

_____

In my relationship with _____ *, I don't*

like _____

_____

_____

This is what I will say or do about it: _____

_____

_____

_____

Don't expect dramatic changes. But telling people what you need and expect from them will help them respect you and not take you for granted.

Besides expressing your own thoughts, communicating in healthy relationships also means listening to the other person. Survivors and teenagers often get defensive when someone criticizes their behavior. Usually when people express annoyance, they are talking about a specific behavior, not about a person's basic nature. The next time people tell you they don't like something you did, listen, ask questions, and pay attention to your own reactions. Are you getting upset? Are you feeling guilty, angry, or defensive? Are they saying that you are bad, or simply that they don't like what you did? If you're unsure of what they meant, ask them. Next, take some time to think about what they said; talk it over with your therapist or a trusted friend. With practice, you won't become so upset or defensive, and you will be able to communicate better.

Developing healthy relationships takes work and patience. Don't be discouraged if the changes come slowly. Keep working at it, and pay attention to the thoughts and feelings you have about yourself and about others. Give yourself permission to make mistakes. People grow and learn throughout their lives. You too will grow and continue to make positive changes.

15

Confronting Your Offender

In a confrontation, you stand up to the person who hurt you and express your feelings. You do not expect validation or support from that person. In fact, that person may blame you or deny the abuse. We are not telling you to confront the offender. We are saying this should be a decision you make carefully with the help of your therapist and other concerned adults. Here are some of the pros and cons.

Confronting can be empowering: you end the secrecy and redirect the blame. Some people confront to inform the family of the extent of the abuse or to break down the abuser's denial. Others confront in order to prevent the offender from abusing other children. Survivors sometimes confront other family members who knew about the abuse but did nothing. They usually do this to express feelings of hurt, anger, or betrayal. Whatever your reasons, when you confront, you have decided that publicly taking a stand is more important than avoiding family conflict.

In confrontations with the offender and/or family members, the survivor often states what he or she expects from that person in the future. Sometimes it's total separation. If survivors choose to have contact, they might outline how they want to be treated. Survivors sometimes ask for partial compensation for the abuse—money for therapy, admission of responsibility to the family, or anything else the survivors feel would help.

Confrontations can be direct or indirect. In a direct confrontation, you speak to your offender face to face or by letter or telephone. An indirect confrontation is symbolic: you say everything you want in role playing or a letter you don't mail, rather than actually to your offender.

The reason for not confronting your offender directly concerns your own safety. Will you be in physical danger by initiating a confrontation? If you were physically hurt during the abuse or if your life or safety was threatened, *do not confront your abuser directly!* Do not consider it if there is any reason to think you might be harmed. Do not even go to other family members who might share the information with the abuser. Some offenders are sociopaths— people without consciences—who are not concerned for anyone else. They want what they want, when they want it, and don't care whom they hurt. They can be extremely dangerous and should be confronted only by the police.

The next consideration is family anger. It is very likely that the person you confront is going to be angry with you. He or she may deny the abuse or call you a liar. You may be blamed for destroying the family. Other family members might also get angry with you. They could say that you are causing trouble or that you should leave the abuse in the past and stop hurting everyone. If you are living at home, don't plan a confrontation with someone who lives in the same house. This could create far too much stress for you. Wait until you are older and independent so that you can leave afterward and not have to go home with your offender! (Although it's best that offenders be removed from the home until they are judged safe, this doesn't always happen. Even with protective services involved, offenders often remain in the household with their victims. If this is your situation, work closely with your therapist to get the support you need.) If the abuse is still going on, tell your therapist or another adult who can help you, or call the child abuse hot line to report it, and arrange for protection before planning any confrontation.

As a teenager, you should plan a direct confrontation only with the help of your therapist. Discuss the potential benefits and the dangers before deciding to go forward. If both of you feel a confrontation will help your recovery, proceed slowly. The next part of this chapter deals with setting up a confrontation, and with the issues and questions that need attention. Use this section to plan an indirect confrontation as well.

Setting Up a Confrontation

This section is divided into groups of questions. Discussing them with your therapist will help you to develop either a direct or a symbolic confrontation that can be empowering for you. The questions will help you sort out your thoughts. Questions in **boldface** type concern what you want to tell or ask your offender.

Before setting up a confrontation, you must have a clear understanding of what it will mean to you and why you think it will be helpful. Then evaluate with your therapist what are fantasies and what are reasonable expectations.

About Confronting

1. What does the word confrontation *mean to you?* _____

_____

_____

_____

2. Why do you want to confront your offender? _____

_____

_____

3. What do you hope your offender will say when confronted?

_____

_____

4. How will you feel if this doesn't happen? _____

_____

_____

5. What do you hope will happen after you confront? _____

_____

_____

_____

6. How will the confrontation help your recovery? _____

_____

_____

_____

7. Why is it important that you take care of yourself now? _____

_____

_____

_____

Your reasons for wanting to confront are important. If you are hoping that this will bring your family together or that your abuser will apologize, you may be sadly disappointed. You need to be prepared for many kinds of reactions and ready to handle them.

Now evaluate your feelings about the abuse and your offender, and decide what you want to say to him or her about it. You need to be clear about your feelings, since telling your offender how you feel is extremely empowering and the main reason for a confrontation.

Feelings About the Abuse

1. How did you feel about yourself during the abuse? _____

_____

_____

_____

2. How did you feel about yourself after the abuse? _____

_____

_____

_____

3. How do you feel about yourself now? _____

_____

_____

4. How do you feel about having been abused? _____

_____

_____

_____

5. How did the abuse affect your life? _____

_____

_____

_____

6. What do you want your offender to know about the way you feel toward yourself? _____

_____

_____

_____

_____

7. What acts of abuse do you specifically want to confront your offender with? _____

_____

_____

_____

_____

8. Why is it important to confront your abuser with these acts?

_____

_____

_____

Feelings Toward Your Offender

1. What feelings do you have toward your offender now? _____

_____

_____

_____

_____

2. What feelings do you want to tell him or her about? _____

_____

_____

_____

3. What got ruined in this relationship because of the abuse?

_____

_____

_____

4. How do you feel about the relationship now? _____

_____

_____

_____

5. What do you want to tell your offender about what was ruined by the abuse? _____

_____

_____

_____

_____

Some survivors want to ask their offenders why the abuse happened or other question(s) related to it. Decide whether there is anything you want to ask for or ask about. You may not get the answer you want, but if you are prepared for that, there is no reason not to ask the questions.

1. What, if anything, do you want to ask your offender about his or her abuse of you? _____

_____

_____

_____

2. Do you want to ask your abuser for anything—an apology, admission of guilt, financial support for therapy—for having abused you? _____

_____

_____

_____

Now that you have thought about a confrontation, look more specifically at your hopes, expectations, fears, and possible reactions.

Emotionally Preparing for the Confrontation

1. How do you expect the confrontation to go? _____

_____

_____

_____

2. How do you want the confrontation to go? _____

_____

_____

_____

3. What do you fear about confronting this person? _____

_____

_____

_____

4. What problems could arise because of it? _____

_____

_____

_____

5. What benefits could come from the confrontation? _____

_____

_____

_____

Your Reactions

1. How will you feel sitting in the same room with your offender?

_____

_____

_____

_____

_____

2. What reactions might you have during the meeting? _____

_____

_____

_____

3. How do you want to behave during the confrontation? _____

_____

_____

_____

4. How do you not want to behave? _____

_____

_____

5. How do you think you will feel afterward? _____

_____

_____

By the time you have gotten to arranging a confrontation, you have already progressed significantly. Take it slowly. You may be surprised at the feelings that come up for you. *You do not have to go through with this if it feels overwhelming.* Go only as far as is comfortable for you. You may choose to postpone or make it an indirect confrontation. That's okay. If you do decide to proceed, consider the support you will want during the actual session.

Support Needed During the Confrontation

1. Who do you want to be there? _____

_____

_____

2. How would you like them to behave? _____

_____

_____

3. Do you want to have anything with you—a teddy bear, special charm, or something else? _____

_____

_____

4. Where do you want the confrontation to be? _____

_____

_____

5. Where will each person sit (who will sit next to you, where will your offender sit, etc.)? _____

_____

_____

6. Is there anything else that will be important to you during it (how you will dress, how your support people will act)? _____

_____

_____

_____

_____

You have now covered most of the significant issues regarding the confrontation. Before actually setting the date, you and your therapist should explore any other concerns that might have come up.

If you decide not to proceed, you have still prepared everything you need to confront your perpetrator indirectly. If you choose this way, it can still be satisfying. Writing a letter to the offender, mailed or not, is a method used by many survivors. Here is an example of such a letter:

> I guess I finally realize this is a much overdue letter. Although being what you are, you don't even deserve this. I guess I owe that all to justice. During these ten years, I think someone forgot to tell me that justice can be cruel and unfair. I mean, look at you, someone who created so much trauma is allowed to walk free. Well, I never will.
>
> I will never walk free from all the guilt, pain, shame, and unforgivable dirtiness. You took advantage of me, a little girl who was trusting and looked to you for protection when my parents were gone. You violated it, you son of a bitch. I was helpless and had no defenses and yet you thrived on it. You violated me mentally, physically, and socially.
>
> What kind of person are you? A person who manipulates and sucks the power out of an innocent girl. You're a sick man, you enjoy touching girls who cry and obviously don't give any consent. You left me feeling dirty and unwanted. You're so disgusting that I seriously think I'm going to be sick.
>
> We trusted you. Me, my parents, all trusted you and you fuckin' did it anyways. Why? Why did you take it all from me? You took my innocence from me before I even knew what innocence was. At the age of five, I had to learn how to be an adult. I had to keep a horrible, shameful secret which almost pushed me to suicide. God knows I wouldn't give you the satisfaction. I learned how to protect families,

mine and yours. Yes yours! I protected them from all the pain that YOU caused. Yes, you did it you bastard. I'll never get my childhood back. It's gone for good. The nightmares will never subside. I remember, and as long as I do, you must live with the fact that you molested me.

People like you, who are self-centered, deserve to be dead. Part of me wants you to be dead and yet the other part wants you to live forever. This way you can live with the guilt and embarrassment. You'll always have to look at the shame in everyone's eyes when they look at you. I kept your secret but not anymore. You're not going to live a normal life anymore. I'm going to make sure your life is just as humiliated as mine has been for the last ten years. My life has been a living hell. You wouldn't even know what it is like to wake up from a nightmare of you and not even be able to go to my own mother. Whether it takes four notes or 50,000 I'll keep writing. I'll never let you forget the abuse you did to me. You're going to have to live with molesting me. I'm tough but you created me. All the strength you took from me, I'm taking back now. I'm never going to let you get away with it.

Yes, you took my strength, my innocence, my pride, my self-esteem and my body and mind. You thrived on intimidation, my fear, and love for my family. But you didn't take my will to survive, I'm still alive. The child in me may be scarred for life and may even be dead. But I still lived and I'm going to make something out of myself. I may never be able to feel again but I do know one thing. In my heart and soul, I know I will get you back and do whatever I can to make you pay.

Following is space to write your own letter. Use more paper if you need it.

_____

_____

_____

_____

_____

_____

_____

_____

_____

_____

_____

_____

_____

_____

_____

_____

_____

Whether you confront directly or indirectly, you will have done a great deal of work. Be proud of yourself.

16

Should I Forgive?

To forgive means "to pardon an offense, to absolve from blame, to stop feeling resentment against someone." Many people believe that forgiving is necessary in order to heal from sexual abuse.

This chapter is about two kinds of forgiveness: forgiving yourself and forgiving your offender. We believe that in order to heal, forgiving yourself is necessary; forgiving your offender is optional. Victims of abuse often think they're guilty of causing it. They think that if they forgive their offenders, they will no longer feel guilty themselves. You can forgive yourself for what happened without having to forgive your offender.

A major step in your healing depends on taking care of and forgiving yourself. Answer these questions:

When I think about the abuse, do I feel guilty about any part of it?

_____ *What part?* _____

_____

_____

_____

_____

_____

_____

Is there anything I could have done differently? _____

What? _____

_____

_____

_____

*Would I expect as much from another child of that age as I expected
from myself?* _____

Did I ask or force [name the offender] _____ *to abuse me?*

What made me believe the abuse was my fault? _____

_____

_____

_____

_____

What did the offender or anyone else have to gain by blaming me?

_____

_____

_____

_____

Who is really at fault for the abuse? _____

_____

In many cases, kids who have been abused feel angry and worthless, and they act on those feelings in ways they later regret. Ac-
knowledging that you wish things had been different is okay; belit-

tling yourself because things weren't will not change anything. You
need to forgive yourself for what you did in the past. You may want
to change some things you're still doing now. Working on these
things is what's important now.

Talk with your therapist about the behaviors you want to change.
Talking about your guilt and shame will help you to get rid of them. If
you are thinking, "I couldn't talk about what I did," write it down and
then take it to therapy or to someone else you trust to talk about it.

Things I wish I hadn't done: _____

_____

_____

_____

_____

_____

_____

You can treat yourself well only if you stop blaming yourself. Only
then will others treat you well.

Since you've come this far, you're already on the road to recovery
and can be proud of yourself. Working with your therapist will help
you to continue down this road.

I'm proud of myself for _____

_____

_____

_____

I'm treating myself well when I _____

_____

_____

_____

A different and separate issue is whether to forgive your offender. Offenders often think that they should be forgiven if they apologize. The real question is, How do you feel? The following questions will help you to decide if forgiving him or her is right for you and, if so, whether this is the best time.

When I think about forgiving my offender, I feel _____

_____

_____

_____

Do you believe that your offender feels remorse (deep and painful regret) for abusing you? This is an important factor in deciding whether to forgive.

I believe my offender is really sorry for abusing me because _____

_____

_____

_____

I don't believe my offender is sorry because _____

_____

_____

_____

If your offender apologized, did it seem sincere to you? _____

_____

_____

When the person who abused me apologized, I felt _____

_____

_____

_____

_____

_____

Is anyone pressuring you to forgive the offender in order to make things pleasant again in the family or in the neighborhood? If this is the case, you may feel reabused because your feelings aren't being respected, and you're again being made responsible for the offender.

I feel pressured to forgive the offender because _____

_____

_____

_____

_____

_____

Your healing does *not* depend on forgiving the offender. Forgiving might help you—or it might not. We aren't telling you not to forgive. We are telling you that you should forgive *only* if and when it feels right for you to do so. You need to pay attention to your feelings about this, *not* to what others want.

I want to forgive my offender because _____

_____

_____

_____

_____

I don't want to forgive my offender because _____

_____

_____

_____

_____

It's natural to have mixed feelings, and it's all right to think about both the reasons why you would and why you wouldn't want to forgive. Not all acts are forgivable, nor are all acts even understandable. Sometimes you can get caught up in trying to make sense out of something that makes no sense. Don't let yourself get too entangled in this question. Right now, you need to put your energy into yourself. Whatever you decide, whether to forgive or not, it's your choice to make. You do have the right to make that choice.

Having Fun

S ome people have trouble enjoying themselves. When you are enjoying yourself, you are either relaxed and comfortable or excited and happy. It sounds easy, doesn't it? Actually, many people, abused or not, have no idea what fun is or how to enjoy themselves. For them, being with other people can be uncomfortable, and doing "fun" things can produce anxiety.

Perhaps you don't seem to enjoy life, or you have little interest in anything. As you get further on in your healing and are no longer focused on the abuse, you'll have room for other things. You will be likely to want more fun and to develop new interests. Fun means play, having a good time: going to the movies, "hanging out," or playing a sport, for example. Some people think they have fun only when they are drinking or drugging. (If you're one of them, we want you to learn to enjoy yourself in healthier ways.)

What do you do for fun now? _____

_____

_____

_____

Do any of those things get you into trouble or cause you problems?

_____*What?* _____

_____

_____

_____

Make a list of activities you think are fun (whether you do them or not). Ask other people what they do, and decide if those things sound good to you. Go over the list with your therapist or friends and put a check next to each thing that could get you into trouble. This will help you to know what is healthy and what is destructive.

_____   _____

_____   _____

_____   _____

_____   _____

_____   _____

_____   _____

There are ways to have fun that you might not know about. The best way to find out what's fun for you is to try new things so you can develop new interests. Some things you try you won't like; others you will. You'll see that as you develop more interests, you'll meet other people who have those same interests.

Getting into new situations and meeting new people can also be frightening. You could be afraid of being ignored or made fun of. These feelings are common, but in many cases, there is little basis for them. Each time you take this risk and succeed, joining in gets a little easier. Eventually you will have a variety of interests, and you'll probably be enjoying life more and making new friends. Perhaps your past friendships were based on mutual problems. Friendships you make now can be based on new interests. Some of these interests and friendships may last throughout your life.

It may be a challenge for you to discover what you like and what you find interesting. Here are some questions to help you explore this.

When you have seen other kids having fun, what were they doing?

_____

_____

Have you ever seen kids having fun and wished you were with them?

_____*What were they doing?* _____

_____

_____

Is there anything you wish you could try? _____

_____

_____

Why do you want to do this? _____

_____

_____

Think about the things you are already interested in; what are they?

_____

_____

_____

As people grow their interests change, and their ideas about what's fun change. Is there anything that used to be fun for you that isn't anymore? _____

_____

_____

_____

As you try new things, thoughts or feelings due to the abuse could intrude, causing you to feel insecure and different. You may think everyone can tell and that they are looking at you strangely. Feeling this way occasionally during the healing process is normal; it happens to many who are recovering from trauma. When old feelings come up, you may feel as though you've gone backward. You haven't. You need to learn to focus on the present and to put your complete attention on the activity that you are now involved in.

We end this chapter with a "future" exercise. Close your eyes, relax, take in some deep breaths, and imagine yourself a year from now, doing something that is fun, feeling confident, and being the person you want to be.

Different Therapies

You can get help, support, and guidance from a variety of therapies. You've probably heard of individual, family, and group therapies. Others include body work, expressive, and sex therapies.

In *individual therapy,* you meet alone with a therapist, usually weekly. You decide together what you want to achieve and how to work toward that goal. In individual therapy, you should feel a closeness and alliance with your therapist that allows you to tell that person things you might not tell anyone else. If you don't feel comfortable with your therapist after working together a while, consider finding someone else. Not every two people are a match, and you have the right to find a match for you.

In *family therapy,* the family meets with the therapist—usually weekly or maybe less frequently. This type of therapy can be a helpful choice because the family as well as the victim often has problems due to the sexual abuse. It also helps the family to understand the part they can play in your healing, as well as the stages everyone will go through during it. In this case, the therapist is working for the good of the entire family rather than for that of one specific member.

In *group therapy,* one or two therapists and a group of clients meet to discuss and work through issues. In a sexual abuse group, the members are typically survivors. These groups may be very structured with clear goals and a time limit, or they may be more flexible. In the groups we run, we expect the members also to be working on the abuse in individual therapy. At the end of this chapter, we include a segment from one of Shari's groups.

Body work therapies are those that use touch and movement as a way of getting to memories and feelings. These include massage, acupuncture, and therapeutic touch.

Expressive therapies use music, art, dance, psychodrama, and/or movement. They help to release the person from blocks that keep them from expressing themselves freely and appropriately.

Sex therapy is an option for adults with problems in their sexual adjustment. Sexual issues are addressed through specific exercises and techniques. Sex therapy is conducted by a trained sex therapist and is usually accompanied by individual therapy.

We recommend that you start with individual therapy and add family and group therapy as soon as you are ready and able. Body work and expressive therapy may be a helpful addition.

Choosing the Right Therapist

In choosing a therapist, first ask yourself how you feel with that person. Is he or she someone you can talk to and who understands you? Is this person knowledgeable and experienced in sexual abuse work? You have every right to inquire. Here are some questions to ask:

1. How long have you worked in the area of sexual abuse?
2. How did you get your training in this area?
3. How do you keep up your knowledge about sexual abuse treatment?
4. How long have you worked with teenagers?
5. Do you ever see the abuse as the child's fault? (If he or she says yes, find someone else)

In choosing a family or group therapist, you will want to know still more. Most family therapists have had additional training or supervised experience working with families. It's a good idea to ask about it. Group therapists should have had experience both running groups and working with survivors. Ask them:

1. How much experience have you had working with families in which sexual abuse was an issue?
2. How much experience have you had running groups?
3. Have you ever run a survivors' group before?

You and your therapist are going to be working very closely together through ups and downs. Make sure the person you choose is right for you.

> If you go to a therapist and this is your first time, meet with him a couple of times to get the feel of the person. See if you're comfortable with him, and if you're not comfortable *do not* stay there! Get out. Each person is different, and each therapist is different, so you need a person that fits you. And you need somebody that you can relate to and talk to. If you don't have that relationship with your therapist, I don't see you getting anything done. You need someone you can really count on and trust. If you've got a funny feeling, you don't just stick with that person and be unhappy. You just go to a different person. Try somebody else. There's always someone that's right for you. (Tina, 16)

A Group Therapy Session

Following is a portion of one group therapy session. The members volunteered to have their sessions taped and included in this book in order to help others. Due to the length of the session, we have included only a portion of their discussion. The group began with members' summaries for the week; then a discussion developed about boyfriends and sex and needing control.

> *Shari:* Do you think it [needing to be in control] has anything to do with having been abused?
>
> *Ann:* I think it has a lot to do with it because I have to be in control all the time. If I'm with a guy and I say no, and I get the slightest hint that he's not going to respect that, then whether I want to do it or not . . . Do you know what I'm talking about?
>
> *Shari:* Do you think things would be different if your life circumstances had been different?
>
> *Ann:* I think I probably wouldn't have such a big deal with control.
>
> *Shari:* Is that just in the area of sex or other areas too?
>
> *Ann:* I have to deal with that in a lot of stuff.
>
> *Skylar:* I feel the same way.

Ann: I'm in a power struggle with my parents. I think I have a right to control my own life and they don't.

Ashley: You want to control all kinds of situations. That's how I am. You want to control what's going on, you know. When it gets out of control, you break down. I break down when I'm not in control.

Ann: I don't know, I just feel like I always have to be in control. I just always feel like I have to be in control of everything. The majority of situations in my life I have to be in control of. If I'm with a guy, I have to be in control. If I'm at home, I have to be in control of what I do. Like, I mean, if my parents say I can't go out, I'll sneak out. Whether it really makes that much difference to me or not, I just want to say, "You can't tell me what I can and can't do. I'm in control of my life. I can do what I want."

Shari: How does that tie in with the abuse?

Ashley: You weren't in control then. You want to be in control now.

Kayla: I want to be in control, but I have a hard time getting control. I feel like I can't get a grip on things. I feel like I'm always out of control and I feel lost.

Ashley: You want to make sure that everyone else sees that you're in control. I was talking to Sam [boyfriend] about this. He said, "You act different when you're in school." And I said, "Well, I have to be a different person in front of everyone. I have to make a good impression and be somebody who I'm not all the time." And he's like, "Well, you act differently toward me." And I'm like, "It's just the way I am, Sam." When we're alone, I'm different. I'm pretty much natural, but I have to be, in everyone else's eyes, perfect. You know, when I'm in school, I have to do everything right.

Ann: I don't have to be perfect. I'm very opposite her perfect. I'm a screw-up.

Skylar: Me too. I hate rules. All the rules in my school I think I've broken a few thousand times.

Shari: How come?

Skylar: Because I hate rules. I hate people telling me what to do. It's none of their fucking business. I can do what I want.

Shari: How come it's so important to not let anyone tell you what to do?

Skylar: Because they'll shit all over you just like everyone else does.

Ann: I have to be in control of what I do. Whether it's breaking rules, I don't care. I mean, if in order to be in control of a situation, I have to break rules, I don't care.

Shari: So you're in control by breaking the rules. And that's how you are, too, Skylar? And you're in control by being perfect—by making sure that everything is exactly the way it's supposed to be, that you look good, that you act good—Is that it?

Ashley: That I'm somebody that everyone else wants me to be most of the time. I don't take any shit, but I want to be what everyone else thinks I should be. I want to be nice and perfect. Like, girls at my school, I want them to envy me, you know. I have nothing for them to envy, but I still want them to envy me, you know. If they had my life, they'd be jumping off cliffs and stuff, you know. But I just want to feel like I'm envied.

Ann: You want them to envy what they think you have.

Ashley: Yeah. See, my vice-principal said to me, I got upset in school one day and I didn't tell him what was going on. I said I had a family problem, and the shit was going to hit the fan pretty much, and I just didn't know when, and I was upset about it. That was when all this started happening, when I found out my mom told everyone. And he said, "See, now I never would have known anything was wrong with you because you're always fine. When you're in school, you act like there's nothing wrong."

Kayla: A lot of people say that to me.

Ashley: "You're perfect. And inside you're really screwed up." Well, not screwed up, but, you know, you're hurting.

Ann: That's the way I was before I went into the hospital, basically. Or about a year ago, probably, before all the shit started to hit the fan. Especially in junior high. I always got straight A's.

Ashley: I was like that when I lived in Pennsylvania. I had to be perfect. My lowest grade was a C and I was highly depressed about that. That was in science.

Shari: (to Kayla) What are you like?

Kayla: I don't know. I want everybody to think I'm fine.

Ashley: But when you get upset, do you want everybody to console you?

Kayla: Yeah, wicked bad. And sometimes I want everybody to know. I want them to be like, "Wow! You went through a lot of shit. I feel bad for you."

Ashley: Yeah. Exactly! You want them to feel sorry for you. Like, with Alice and Nicole, [friends] I wanted them to feel guilty. I wanted them to see I've been through enough shit. I don't need theirs too. But, I don't know, there's some things we can and can't do. I feel bad about that sometimes. Wanting them to know all the shit I've been through.

Kayla: I feel bad about that too.

Ashley: It's not something just anyone should know. It's like, it's wrong to want them to feel bad for you. I feel like it's wrong.

Shari: Why is it wrong to want people to feel badly for you about what happened? You did go through a lot.

Ashley: Well, you want them to like you for what you are, not for what happened to you.

Kayla: You want recognition.

Shari: You think that they should like you because you had bad experiences?

Ashley: No, but, in a way you want them more sympathetic. They'll be nice to you because of what happened. And sometimes you want that, but when everything is fine with you, you want them to be cool to you . . .

We end this book with advice from some of the survivors who shared their stories:

Hold onto your inner strength. Don't let anything stop you from letting it out. And if you feel sad or have any problems, talk it over with a parent or an adult you trust, a therapist. Just let it out. And if you have to cry, cry. (Michael, 13)

I would say stick to dealing with it and stay in therapy because it's the best thing for you. You can't go wrong doing that because you've got to stay on that track and keep going. No matter how hard it gets, just keep going and keep facing it. It can only help you, as hard as it may seem and as much as it may hurt you. It can make you a stronger person, and it will better your relationships. You shouldn't be afraid of how you feel. It's not your fault. (Tina, 16)

If you can handle taking the person to court, if that would help resolve everything, that's great. Then do it and don't let anything stop you if your heart's in it. But if you're not comfortable with it or you just don't want anyone else to know, go to a counselor or tell your parents. Your parents have a right to know, because you're their child and they should know. Sometimes, you just get in a mood and you just react badly to everything and it's because of the abuse. So, if you lash out at your parents, sometimes you can get in trouble. And sometimes they're hurt. So I think it's just right to tell your parents. If your parent's the abuser, then tell your other parent. Or, if you don't have another parent, tell an older sibling or go to the Department of Social Services, or someone that can help you. (Ashley, 17)

I guess my advice right off would be not to think it's going to be handled right overnight. That was one of my biggest things. I thought I was going to go in the hospital and life would be great after that. It's four years later now and I'm still dealing with it. So, I guess first off I'd say, Don't think it's going to get done overnight. Which isn't to say that good things don't happen as you go. I mean, I look at myself now and I see so much of a difference that it's just amazing to me, but at the same time, don't get your hopes too high because it's real hard to come to grips with it. But, other than that, I say get help even if you can't tell your parents or someone around you. Still go get help because it's doable.

It gets me so mad when I see victims go out and do it to someone else. I think that's disgusting. There's no excuse for that in my mind. If you know it happened to you, then it's your responsibility to get help even if you feel all funny, if you feel weak and stuff, that's still no excuse. To me the biggest reason is so that you won't do it to anybody else. There's a lot of good things that come out of getting help for that reason.

I see people wasting their lives all the time because the person that abused them is still abusing them, even if they're not around. You can always get help from centers and stuff. There's always a way. There's always going to be somebody that you can go to. (Paula, 19)

Get help right away. It doesn't matter who you talk to. I mean, the more you put it off, the harder it's going to be for you. You know, not just hard to talk about, but hard on everyone, especially on yourself. Not being able to communicate, being so afraid of everything, not trusting. I think that's probably the key word; trusting. But the first step is, you need to talk to someone and it needs to be someone that you trust, you know, a trusted friend, a family member, the sooner the better.

It probably won't change instantly. It's going to take time to heal the wounds that you have. And I would tell them to go into therapy. It did a lot of good for me. I have to take some control of my life because before it was always, like, agreeing with everybody. (Jimmy, 23)

For Your Parents

This chapter was written to address your parents' issues about, and reactions to, your abuse. Read it over and decide if it would be helpful to you if they were to read it. If so, cut it out and give it to them.

F ew things are more painful than finding out that your child was hurt and that you are powerless to take the pain away. Helping your child to recover from sexual abuse will be a long and difficult process for everyone involved. It's important for you to take care of yourself so you have the energy to care for others too. These things can help: emotional support from caring friends or family members; therapy groups for parents of sexually abused children;* and parents' support groups (if none is available, you can start one). There are also self-help books for parents of sexually abused children; refer to the recommended readings at the end of the book.

Many feelings may arise from your learning about the abuse. You may feel guilty for not having been aware that it was happening. You may blame yourself for not having anticipated it. Such feelings are not unusual, although they may not always be realistic.

If a family member or close friend is the offender, your feelings may be quite confused. You may find your loyalties split. Families sometimes take sides, creating still more losses for you and your child. If the offender is a sibling, you may feel torn apart. How do you choose between two of your children? How do you make sense out of what happened? Your potential sense of guilt could

---

*These can generally be found through local mental health centers, or from the sexual abuse hot line, 1-800-422-4453.

be so great that you don't want to believe your child. If you feel this way, talk with a trained counselor. It is necessary to support your victimized child; you may need help in giving it.

If the offender was one of your parents, it may bring up memories of your own past abuse or confusion about loyalties. This issue needs to be dealt with separately from your child's abuse. You have to address your child's needs first, but you will need to deal with your own abuse as well.

If the offender is your spouse, the issues are even more complex. Your entire way of life, and your child's, could be changed, especially if you depend solely on your spouse's income. You also have to come to terms with the fact that you were betrayed by someone you love and trusted. You may be surprised to find you still love this person; you don't automatically stop loving someone, no matter how angry and disappointed you might be. You may find it easier to be angry with your child than with your spouse. It may, in fact, become easier to believe your spouse than your child because of everything at stake. Believe your child. Children do not normally lie about these things; offenders usually do.

When a child has been abused, especially by a parent, that child usually takes on a caretaking role with the offender and with the rest of the family. Children are often unable to give up this role while living with the offender, and treatment in many cases is ineffective. For this reason, we believe that the child should not have to live with or have contact with the offender until that person takes responsibility for the abuse and is in treatment. We strongly advise that the offender, *not* the child, leave the household. Children who are taken from their homes feel blamed. Forcing children to leave causes them to feel abandoned and to feel reabused. We realize this may be an extremely difficult choice for you, but at this time your child's well-being and future lie in the balance.

Families handle parental abuse in different ways. Many split up; some choose to reunite. If you as a parent want to work toward reunification, this should be done in a slow and thoughtful manner with the help of trained professionals and law enforcement and child welfare agencies.

Parents sometimes think that other children in the family can be protected from knowing about the abuse, but children always know when something important and unbalancing is happening to a family. When the family is in emotional upheaval, pretending nothing is wrong is very frightening for children. What to tell the other children, and how to tell them, will depend on their ages. Parents usually find therapy for themselves and their families helpful with deciding about disclosure.

Sexually abused children act out in a variety of ways—truancy, sexual promiscuity, running away, and compulsive/addictive behaviors. They are trying to block the pain. Some become overly compliant, or they become overachievers. While this may seem like a good adjustment to adults, it is likely to be a brittle one; their egos may be easily shattered. When things don't work out— failing a test, plans not coming through—they can fall apart. Notice whether your child's reactions are out of proportion to a situation; notice whether he or she frequently becomes inconsolable.

People who have been sexually abused are usually diagnosed as having post-traumatic stress disorder. Compulsive/addictive behaviors are often part of this syndrome. The symptoms can be delayed for years, emerging only when a stressful event occurs. The event is often unrelated to the abuse, but it arouses similar feelings of hopelessness, helplessness, and loss. Sometimes memories of the abuse are forgotten, and they are recalled only when the victim is strong enough to deal with them. Some parents find the issue of sexual abuse so painful that they deny its effects. They look to other causes for the problems their child is having, preferring to link those problems to a more recent event. When this happens, the child is discouraged from dealing with the pain, shame, and despair caused by the abuse; his or her compulsive/addictive behaviors get treated on the level of symptoms instead of root causes.

Children who were sexually abused often become angry with a nonoffending parent. They feel enraged for not having been protected. While it is true that they weren't protected, the reality may be that there was no way this parent could have known. But feelings have little to do with logic. Children don't always know why they feel so angry, and that can make them feel even worse. It's important for you to understand what is happening. If you put it in perspective and don't overreact, these trying times could go more smoothly. We aren't suggesting you allow your children to become abusive. We simply mean that when feelings are explosive, children need some space. You can talk later, when you are both calmer.

Children need consistency and understanding to work through this issue. Our advice is much easier said than done. Being sexually abused makes your child feel badly about himself or herself. It's often easier for both you and your child to feel anger than to feel the pain and helplessness associated with abuse. Your children usually know you very well, and they know how to aggravate you. Consciously reminding yourself of this can make it easier not to overreact.

Having a support system in place will give you an outlet for your feelings. A therapist could be helpful through the rough spots. Even with everything in place, dealing with sexual abuse is very painful for most parents. Time, understanding, and hard work are the best healers.

Resources

Hot Lines and Information Telephone Numbers

- National Child Abuse Help Hotline
  1-800-422-4453
  For information or if you were abused
- National Self-Help Clearinghouse
  1-212-642-2944
  Listings of self-help groups throughout the country
- National AIDS Hotline
  1-800-342-AIDS
  1-800-344-SIDA
  Spanish-speaking operators available for information and referral
- National Sexually Transmitted Disease Hotline
  1-800-227-8922
  For information and referral
- National Runaway Hotline
  1-800-231-6946
  If you are on the run or are thinking about it, call for help first.
  The primary goal is to help kids find a safe place to stay.
- Cocaine Hotline
  1-800-COCAINE
  1-800-262-2463
  Answers questions and provides referrals
- Al-Anon Family Group Headquarters
  1-800-356-9990
  Provides information about groups in your area
- National Suicide Hotline
  1-800-666-9155

- Trained counselors available on confidential help line, first answered by a recorded message; stay on the line and a counselor will pick up
- Incest Survivors Anonymous
P.O. Box 5613
Long Beach, CA 90805-0613
1-213-428-5599
Provides information on self-help groups nationwide

These numbers are called frequently, so it may take a while for them to answer. Be patient, and stay on the line.

Recommended Readings for Teens

Bell, Ruth. *Changing Bodies, Changing Lives: A Book for Teens About Sex and Relationships.* New York: Random House, 1980.

Cole, Autumn, and Becca Brin Manlove. *Brother-Sister Sexual Abuse: It Happens and It Hurts, A Book for Sister Survivors.* Virginia, Minn.: Beccautumn Books, 1991. (c/o Sexual Assault Program of Northern St. Louis County, 505 12th Avenue West, Virginia, Minneapolis, 55792.)

Daugherty, Lynn B. *Why Me? Help for Victims of Child Sexual Abuse, (Even If They Are Adults Now).* Racine, Wis.: Mother Courage Press, 1984.

Davis, Laura. *The Courage to Heal Workbook.* New York: Harper & Row, 1990.

Evert, Kathy, and Inie Bijkerk. *When You're Ready: A Woman's Healing from Childhood Physical and Sexual Abuse by Her Mother.* Walnut Creek, Calif.: Launch Press, 1988.

Gil, Eliana. *United We Stand: A Book for People with Multiple Personalities.* Walnut Creek, Calif.: Launch Press, 1990.

———. *Outgrowing the Pain: A Book for and About Adults Abused as Children.* Walnut Creek, Calif.: Launch Press, 1983.

Grubman-Black, Stephen. *Broken Boys/Mending Men: Recovery from Child Sexual Abuse.* Blue Ridge Summit, Penn.: Tab Books, 1990.

Hamilton, Eleann. *Sex, with Love: A Guide for Young People.* Boston: Beacon Press, 1978.

Irwin Smith, Lucinda. *Growing Up Female: New Challenges, New Choices.* New York: Julian Messner, 1987.

King County Rape Relief. *Top Secret: Sexual Assault Information for Teenagers Only.* 1985. (305 South 43d, Renton, Washington 98055.)

Narimanian, Rosemary. *Secret Feelings and Thoughts: A Book About Male Sexual Abuse.* Healing Hearts, 1990. (Philly Kids Play It Safe, 1421 Arch St., Philadelphia, Pennsylvania 19102-1582.)

Powell, Elizabeth. *Talking Back to Sexual Pressure*. Minneapolis: Comp Care Publishers, 1991.

Seixas, Judith S. *Living with a Parent Who Drinks Too Much*. New York: Greenwillow Books, 1979.

Recommended Reading for Parents

Adams, Caren, Jennifer Fay, and Jan Loreen-Martin. *NO Is Not Enough: Helping Teenagers Avoid Sexual Assault*. San Luis Obispo, Calif.: Impact Publishers, 1984.

Bateman, Py, and Gayle Stringer. *Where Do I Start? A Parents' Guide for Talking to Teens About Acquaintance Rape*. Dubuque, Iowa: Kendall-Hunt Publishing, 1984.

Byerly, Carolyn. *The Mother's Book: How to Survive the Incest of Your Child*. Dubuque, Iowa: Kendall-Hunt Publishing, 1985.

Hagans, Kathryn, and Joyce Case. *When Your Child Has Been Molested*. Lexington Books, New York, N.Y. 1988.

Sanford, Linda. *The Silent Children: A Parents' Guide to the Prevention of Child Sexual Abuse*. New York: McGraw-Hill, 1980.

Bibliography

Bass, Ellen, and Davis, Laura. *The Courage to Heal.* New York: Harper & Row, 1988.

Blume, E. Sue. *Secret Survivors: Uncovering Incest and Its Aftereffects in Woman.* New York: John Wiley and Sons, 1989.

Courtois, Christine A. *Healing the Incest Wound: Adult Survivors in Therapy.* New York: W. W. Norton & Co., 1988.

Dolan, Yvonne. *Resolving Sexual Abuse.* New York: W. W. Norton & Co., 1991.

Finkelhor, David. *Child Sexual Abuse: New Theory and Research.* New York: The Free Press, 1984.

Herman, Judith. *Father-Daughter Incest.* Cambridge: Harvard University Press, 1981.

Kluft, Richard P., ed. *Incest Related Syndromes of Adult Psychopathology.* Washington, D.C.: American Psychiatric Press, 1990.

Lew, Michael. *Victims No Longer: Men Recovering from Incest and Other Sexual Child Abuse.* Nevraumony Publishing, 1988.

Putnam, Frank W. *Diagnosis and Treatment of Multiple Personality Disorder.* New York: Guilford Press, 1989.

Ross, Colin A. *Multiple Personality Disorder.* New York: John Wiley & Sons, 1989.

Index

— A —

Abuse. *See* Cult abuse; Drugs and substance abuse; Effects of sexual abuse; Physical abuse; Ritual abuse; Sexual abuse
Aggravated sexual play, 63
AIDS, 72
Alcoholism and drinking, 19, 35, 61, 62, 127
Anger, xvii, 22, 29
  in confrontations, 108
  in families, 33, 108
  at nonoffending parent, 141
  in post-traumatic stress disorder, 14
Anxiety/panic attacks, 12, 14, 73, 127

— B —

Blanking out. *See* Dissociation
Boundaries
  creation of, 5, 7
  defined, xv
  in families, 33
  personal limits, xv, 5, 6–7
  violation of, 71

— C —

Child abuse hot lines, 3–4, 54, 108
Child molestation, 62
Child welfare agencies, 140
Chronic illness, 35
Church groups, 39
Compulsive/addictive behavior, 19–20, 141
Concentration, lack of, 12–13, 14
Confrontation, 80
  avoidance of, 5
  dangers of, 108
  direct, 107–108
  emotional preparation for, 114
  feelings about the abuse, 110–12
  feelings toward the offender, 112–13
  indirect (symbolic), 107–109
  letter writing, 107, 117–18
  power gained from, 107, 110
  reactions to, 115
  reasons for, 110
  setting up, 108–110
  support during, 116–17
  therapist-guided, 108, 117

Control
 of feelings, 20
 need for, 133–34, 135, 138
Coping skills, 15–23
Criticism, 106
Cult abuse, xiv–xv, 50–51

— D —

Date rape, 12, 26
Defense mechanisms, 15–
 23
Defensive behavior, 106
Denial
 of abuse, 18
 family dysfunction and, 38
 of feelings, 6
 by offender, 64
 by parents, 90, 141
Department of Social Services,
 137
Depression, xvii, 19, 21
 blamed for abusive behavior, 62
 suicidal thoughts and, 24
Disclosure, 90–91
 to family, 54, 90–91
 as healing process, 82–84,
  85–89
 of incest, 54, 90
 therapist-guided, 91
 reactions to, 90
 risks of, 88
 to therapist, 83–84
Dissociation, 14, 21
 as coping mechanism, 16–
  18, 82
 by offender, 63

Divorce, 33
Drugs and substance abuse,
 19, 20, 35, 61, 127
 blamed for abusive behavior, 62
Dysfunctional families, 9, 30–
 31, 35–37, 39–40
 mistakes and perfectionism
  in, 40–41, 43
 questionnaire, 36–37
 rules in, 42, 43
 secrets in, 39
 sexual abuse outside the
  family and, 42

— E —

Eating disorders, 20, 21
Effects of sexual abuse, xiii,
 xv, 9–13, 51
 coping and defense mechanisms, 15–23
 post-traumatic stress disorder, 14–15
 on sexuality, 73–75
 symptoms, 20–22
Erections, 68, 70

— F —

Family
 anger in, 33, 108
 behavior of adults, 34–35, 39
 boundaries, 33
 compromises in, 31–32
 defined, 3–4
 development, 30, 31
 extended, 51

parental support of abused
children, 139–40
parenting skills, 32, 33–34
rules, 30, 35
sibling rivalry, 32–33
single-parent, 32
stress in, 31
therapy, 131, 132, 141
See also Dysfunctional families; Incest
Fathers as offenders. *See* Incest
Fear, xvii, 12, 13
Food, 19, 20, 21
Flashbacks, 12, 13, 14–15, 73
Forgiveness
of mistakes, 97–99
of offender, 121, 124–26
pressure for, 125
of yourself, 121–23
Foster homes, 39–40
Friendship, 75, 95, 128
Fun, enjoyment of life, 127–30

— G —

Gender
attitudes toward abuse, xiv
identity, 69, 70
Grandparents as offenders,
51–52, 140
Guilt and shame, 85
in dysfunctional families, 40
of incest, 45
of parents, 139–40
in post-traumatic stress disorder, 14
self-esteem and, 9

for sexual abuse outside the
family, 56–57

— H —

Healing, 130
disclosing abuse to others,
82–84, 85–88
forgiveness, 121–26
having fun, 127–30
memory work, 82–83
risks of disclosure and, 88
stages, 79–81
See also Self-esteem
Hearing noises or voices, 21, 22
Heart problems, 5
Heterosexuality, 70
Homosexuality, 24, 31, 70, 72

— I —

Incest, 15, 61
abuse disguised as caretaking, 53, 60, 140
defined, xiv
disclosure of, 54, 90
extended family offenders,
51
grandparents as offenders,
51–52, 140
parents/stepparents as offenders, 52–54, 60, 140
questionnaire, 45–50
removal of offender from
home, 108, 140
sibling offenders, 52, 139
Independence, 25
Insecurity, 19

— J —

Journals and diaries, xi, 7, 29, 82

— L —

Letter writing, 107
  sample, 117–18

— M —

Masturbation, 68, 73
Memory
  blockage of abuse, 15, 16, 18, 19, 82
  problems, 14
  remembering the abuse, 80, 82–83
  work, in healing, 82–83
Minimizing the abuse, 18
Mistakes, 40–41, 43, 106
  forgiving, 97–99
Mothers as offenders. *See* Incest
Multiple personality, 18

— N —

Nightmares and dreams, 12–13, 14, 15, 22
Numbness, lack of feeling, 10, 21
  as coping mechanism, 16
  family stress and, 35
  in post-traumatic stress disorder, 14

— O —

Offenders
  abused (generational pattern of abuse), 50, 63
  avoid being alone with, 5
  common myths about, 60–61
  continued abuse of others, 137–38
  defined, xiv
  in the family. *See* Incest
  female, 60
  juvenile, 63–64
  male, 60
  outside the family, 42, 55–59
  rationalism by, 62, 63, 64
  strangers as, 55, 61
See also Confrontation
Orgasm, 70
Over- and under-achievement, 40–41, 141. *See also* Perfectionism

— P —

Paranoia, 22
Parents
  discussion for, 139–42
  as offenders, 52–54, 140
Pedophilia, 55, 61
Peer(s)
  pressure about sex, 69, 74
  recognition by, 136
Perfectionism, 19–20, 22, 134, 135, 136
  in dysfunctional families, 40–41

Perpetrators. *See* Offenders
Personal limits. *See* Boundaries
Physical abuse, 29, 35, 73
Post-traumatic stress disorder
    (PTSD), 14–15, 141
Power
    abuser over victim, 61, 72
    of confrontation, 107
    in family, 134
    victim (regaining of power),
        86–87
    violence and, 63
Pregnancy, 72
Promiscuity, 11, 22, 61, 71–
    72, 74, 141
PTSD. *See* Post-traumatic
    stress disorder

— R —

Rape, 12, 61
    date, 12, 26
Rationalization by offenders,
    62, 63, 64
Recognition by peers, 136
Relationships, healthy, 80
    behavior with others, 100–
        103
    communication of feelings,
        104–106
    criticism and, 106
    self-esteem and, 100
    suggestions for change, 103–
        104
    trust in, 10–11, 70, 75
Relaxation exercises, 5–6, 83
Religious/satanic cults, xiv–
    xv, 50–51

Responsibility, 9
    acceptance of, 64
    of adult/abuser, 56, 63, 71
    in families, 36
    victim is never at fault, 45,
        56–57, 62, 71, 80
Risk-taking behavior, 10
Ritual abuse, xiv–xv, 50–
    51
Rule(s)
    breaking, 134–135
    family, 30, 35, 42, 43

— S —

Safety network/support sys-
    tem, xvii, 80, 83, 142
    choice of people for, 3–5
Safety precautions, 5–8, 59
Secrecy/conspiracy of silence,
    56–59, 71, 80
    breaking, 85
    confrontation and, 107
    See also Confrontation;
        Talking about sexual
        abuse
Seductive behavior, 63, 71
Self-esteem/self-image, 9, 21,
    68, 69, 80, 142
    defined, 92, 96–97
    forgiving your mistakes, 97–
        99
    healthy relationships and,
        100
    improvement exercises, 93–
        96
Self-help books, 39, 139
Self-mutilation, 19–20, 21

Sex
  as coping strategy, 19
  effect of sexual abuse on,
    73–75
  fear of, 72
  heterosexual relations, 70
  homosexual relations, 24,
    31, 70
  oral, 73
  peer pressure about, 69, 74
  performance or competence
    worries, 26, 27
  problems with, 11–12
  promiscuity, 11, 22, 61, 71–
    72, 74, 141
  therapy, 131, 132
Sex education, 69
  abuse disguised as, 62, 64
Sexual abuse
  as addiction, 63, 64
  compensation for, 107, 113
  covert, xiii–xiv, 53
  in family. See Incest
  fear of abusing others, 13
  generational pattern of, 50,
    63
  outside the family, 42, 55–59
  overt, xiii, 53, 64
  physical/sexual response to,
    45, 70–71
  preconditions for, 62
  by strangers, 55, 61
  subtle beginning of, 56–57, 64
  victim blamed for, 45, 56–
    57, 58, 71, 80
  See also Disclosure; Effects
    of sexual abuse
Sexual behavior and develop-
    ment, 63, 64

Sexuality
  confusion about, 24, 26–27,
    70
  defined, 68
  development of, 68–69
  gender identity, 69, 70
  hypersexuality, 71–72
  See also Promiscuity
Shame. See Guilt and shame
Sibling rivalry, 32–33
Sleep disorders, 14
Social groups, 39
Sociopathology, 63, 108
Stress, 5, 83
  abuse blamed on, 62–63
  family, 31
Substance abuse, 19, 20, 35,
    61, 62, 127
Suicide/suicidal thoughts, 20,
    21, 24–25, 57
Support system. See Safety net-
    work/support system
Survivors, 9, 10
  defined, xiv
  fear of abusing others, 13
  first-stage, xiv
  guilt and shame, 9, 14, 40,
    45, 85
  second-stage, xiv

— T —

Talking about sexual abuse,
    xvi–xvii, 80
  as healing process, 82–84,
    85–88
  incest, 54, 90
  as therapy for post-trau-
    matic stress syndrome, 15

Telephone hot lines, 3–4, 29, 54
Therapy, xi, 39, 80, 137, 138, 142
  behavioral, 123
  body work, 131, 132
  confrontation counseling, 108, 117
  choice options, 132–33
  dealing with mistakes, 99
  disclosure counseling, 91
  expressive, 131, 132
  family, 131, 132, 141
  goal of, xi
  group, 27, 131, 132, 133–36
  healing process and, 83
  individual, 64, 131
  juvenile offender groups, 64
  for parents of sexually abused children, 139
  relationship with therapist, 42
  sex, 131, 132
  sharing details of the abuse, 83–84
Torture, 73
Trust
  fear of, 10–11
  lack of, 22, 42, 70
  of people in safety network, 4, 138
  in relationships, 10–11, 70, 75

— U —

Ulcers, 5

— V —

Venereal disease, 72
Victim
  blamed for abuse, 45, 56–57, 58, 71, 80
  defined, xiv
  guilt felt by, 121, 123
  need for peer recognition, 136
Violence, 63, 73

— W —

Withdrawal, emotional, 14. *See also* Numbness, lack of feeling
Worthlessness, feeling of, 21, 40